MAVERICK

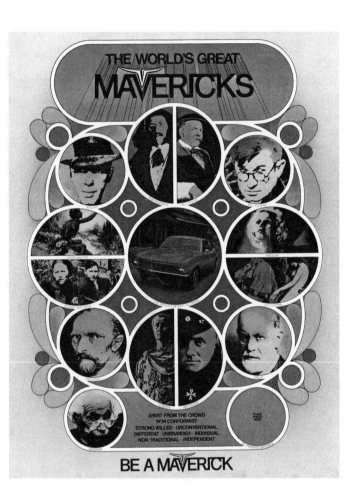

MAVERICK

The American Name That Became a Legend

Lewis F. Fisher

Trinity University Press
SAN ANTONIO, TEXAS

Frontis: A Ford poster promoting the debut of its Maverick compact in 1969 included Sam Maverick, top center left, restyled as a hipster of the 1960s. Others among "The World's Great Mavericks" are, clockwise from the right of his image, W. C. Fields, Will Rogers, Jean Harlow, Lady Godiva, Sigmund Freud, the Red Baron, Julius Caesar, Albert Einstein, Vincent Van Gogh, Bonnie and Clyde, Adam and Eve, and Humphrey Bogart.

Published by Trinity University Press
San Antonio, Texas 78212

Copyright © 2017 by Lewis F. Fisher

Book design by Bookmatters
Cover image: © 1898 by Detroit Photographic Co.

ISBN 978-1-59534-842-5 hardback
ISBN 978-1-59534-838-8 paperback
ISBN 978-1-59534-839-5 ebook

Trinity University Press strives to produce its books using methods and materials in an environmentally sensitive manner. We favor working with manufacturers that practice sustainable management of all natural resources, produce paper using recycled stock, and manage forests with the best possible practices for people, biodiversity, and sustainability. The press is a member of the Green Press Initiative, a nonprofit program dedicated to supporting publishers in their efforts to reduce their impacts on endangered forests, climate change, and forest-dependent communities.

The paper used in this publication meets the minimum requirements of the American National Standard for Information Sciences—Permanence of Paper for Printed Library Materials, ANSI 39.48–1992.

CIP data on file at the Library of Congress

21 20 19 18 17 | 5 4 3 2 1

CONTENTS

PREFACE

Who shot Liberty Valance?

In the western movie classic *The Man Who Shot Liberty Valance*, Jimmy Stewart plays Ransom Stoddard, who gets credit for shooting the villain. John Wayne plays the character who actually fired the fatal shot. Ransom Stoddard rises to fame and high position after the event but finally confesses the truth to a reporter. The reporter, Maxwell Scott, realizing that Stoddard's stature was based on a myth, throws his notes into the fire.

"You're not going to use the story, Mr. Scott?" Stoddard asks.

"No, sir," the reporter replies. "This is the West, sir. When the legend becomes fact, print the legend."

Jimmy Stewart could have been playing Sam Maverick, a real-life Texan justifiably noted in his own time but whose latter-day fame is based on legends as stubborn to shed as Ransom Stoddard's. No amount of truth-telling about the word *maverick* seems to have slowed those who enjoy regaling others with the tall tales, especially in the West, where the word originated.

So this book is a whodunit. Who said what to whom unfolds in a story that becomes a historical epic—a telling of the man who unwittingly inspires the word, of cowboys who spread it, of those who get puzzled over it, those who key off its sense of rakishness and independence, and those who make it a factor in presidential elections. Ironically, given its meaning as unbranded, maverick as a brand name has gone viral worldwide.

I like to think I'm no Maxwell Scott. I may have gone west, but I'm from the East, where my journalism training taught me that printing not legend but facts is what you're supposed to do. My wife's family happens to offer a great opportunity to address the consequences of Scott's type of western journalism.

Mary is a Maverick, a great-great-granddaughter of Sam Maverick, whose unbranded cattle led to the origin of the word and to any number of stories why. Mary's parents sent her to the University of Texas, close to home, so she wouldn't marry a Yankee. But San Antonio's military bases constantly bring in people from everywhere else. When I came to Lackland Air Force Base for officer training, I was eager to get off the base. I heard that Mary's grandmother Maverick liked to meet long-lost relatives, even though I'm not kin on the Maverick side, so I called her up. She invited me to dinner to meet her granddaughter—my sixth cousin once removed, a senior at UT and a redhead. I was smitten but got sent overseas. We kept in touch.

Four years later my Air Force stint ended, and we were married and soon settled in San Antonio. I started as a daily newspaper reporter, we began a suburban weekly and added others, then got into regional book publishing. So I had distractions from taking on the maverick case. Plus, who would trust an in-law with doing an objective story? But I'd always been intrigued by outsiders' astonishment at hearing that the word *maverick* came from an actual family, that one of its members had originated another word—*gobbledygook*—and that the family had a tangential relationship with a third word, *lynch*.

And I was still amazed by a comment from left field when, as a newlywed, I was getting my master's in journalism at Columbia University. We had an assignment to find and interview someone of note. I took a shortcut and picked Mary's cousin Ed Maverick, an interior architect who'd worked on some of the tallest new buildings in New York. My story mentioned he'd been born in Texas but went into little family background. It came back from my professor with a good grade and a note: "Perhaps you couldn't be expected to know about the incredible family of Mavericks in Texas, politicians with conscience."

So, I realized, this was a family that intrigued both those who hadn't heard about it and those, even far away, who had. And it was a family with a patriarch burdened with all manner of oft-repeated myths. There was, indeed, a story here.

The Mavericks maintain a strong sense of identity but usually manage not to take themselves too seriously. I found them to be generally outgoing, articulate, inquisitive, and unpretentious, with a refreshing strain of quirkiness. I was advised early on that all Maverick women were artists and all the men were outspoken. One got by just fine as long as one did not call patriarch Sam Maverick a cattle thief. I learned why: countless writers had sworn through the years that he was a rancher who branded all the unbranded cattle he could find. But he didn't, and he wasn't a rancher, either.

I've benefited from the Mavericks' propensity for saving important papers and their willingness to make them accessible. The Maverick Family Papers at the University of Texas at Austin's Briscoe Center for American History include a remarkably deep assortment of papers of Sam and Mary Maverick, contributed by several branches of the family and reaching nearly twelve linear feet. UT's Maury Maverick Sr. Collection exceeds forty-seven linear feet. Through the years my wife's late mother, Jane Maverick McMillan, accumulated an eclectic assortment of family memorabilia and helpful articles. Ellen Maverick Clements Dickson graciously turned me loose in her room of books and albums filled with references to the Maverick family.

I am especially grateful to my wife, Mary, for her objective and valuable critiques; to historians Paula Mitchell Marks, author and editor of several books on the Maverick family, and Mary Margaret McAllen, for her knowledge of the Texas range; to Bruce M. Shackelford, curator of the Witte Museum's South Texas Heritage Center, who deals with Texas every day; to Trinity University Press director Tom Payton—whose puppy is a terrier mix named Maverick—for his enthusiastic encouragement; and to my granddaughter Christina Jane Fisher, eleven, a sixth-generation descendant of Sam Maverick, for pointing out the connection with Harry Potter that wound up ending chapter 10.

ONE

Will the Real Sam Maverick Please Stand Up?

Among favorite tales of America's Old West are conjectures on how the word *maverick* came about. All agree it had something to do with cattle owned by one Sam Maverick. From there things go amok rather quickly.

For openers, will the real Sam Maverick please stand up?

+ Cattle thief. (*St. Louis Republic*, 1888)

+ Texas rancher who believed branding cattle was cruelty to animals. (William Safire, *New York Times*, 2008)

+ A runaway from South Carolina who branded all the wild cattle he could find and ended up with more cattle than anyone else in Texas. (Anson Mills, *My Story*, 1918)

+ Chicken-hearted old rooster who wouldn't brand any of his cattle and returned from the Civil War to find them roaming over a thousand hills. (Charles Siringo, *A Texas Cow Boy*, 1885)

+ Legendary nonconformist who broke the code of the West by refusing to brand his calves. (James Seitz, *Wall Street Journal*, 1983)

+ A very wealthy and influential German who believed not branding his cattle would save labor costs. (*Chicago Republican*, 1867)

+ An old Frenchman who built up a large cattle herd by each year branding fifty yearlings for every one he actually owned. (Joseph G. McCoy, *Historic Sketches of the Cattle Trade*, 1874)

+ A New Englander who resettled near San Antonio in what is now Maverick County to become a cattle rancher. After winning a herd of cattle in a poker game he decided not to brand them, as the custom was, but to let them loose and free on the range. (Kyle Gann, American Public Media, 2016)

+ Texas cattleman and assistant treasurer of the Confederacy who wouldn't brand his cattle. (*Ford Times*, 1969)

+ Lawyer who refused to brand his cattle. (*Wiktionary*, 2016)

+ Engineer and rancher who did not brand his cattle. (*Oxford Dictionaries*, 2016)

+ Owner of three thousand head of cattle, largest herd in all the country. (*Americanisms: The English of the New World*, 1872)

+ Reluctant owner of four hundred head of cattle. (J. Frank Dobie, *The Longhorns*, 1941)

+ Largest cattleman in Texas, with such a large range he could hardly get over it in one season to brand his calves. (Dan Roberts, *Rangers and Sovereignty*, 1914)

The real Sam Maverick, shown in a portrait by Carl von Iwonski, left a name legacy that has confused generations of users of the word.

✦ Sam Maverick was never in Texas in his life. He lived in Puritan Massachusetts. (John Gould, *Christian Science Monitor*, 1987)

Were he still with us, Sam Maverick would not yet be standing up.

No matter how impressive the source, each description above is wrong, some more so than others. The prize for creativity goes to the confection in Kyle Gann's essay "American Mavericks" on American Public Media's website that moves Sam Maverick from the wrong region to the wrong county and imagines him as a poker player. Gann's piece was about maverick American composers, those who did not fit easily into American culture. Like so many who write about one kind of maverick or another, he seems to have felt obliged to include something on Sam Maverick, whose name he at least spelled correctly.[1]

Runner-up is the prolific Maine writer and columnist John Gould's flat denial that Sam Maverick was a Texan. He must have been wearing the blinders that make so many New Englanders oblivious to life west of the Hudson River, for he believed the only possible Sam Mavericks were the historic ones by that name who lived east of the Hudson. Gould insisted that use of the word *maverick* spread from, of all things, the term for an unmarked log in a Maine river drive.[2]

Maverick has evolved as a noun, from being just an unbranded stray calf to a nonconforming person to an extreme of "an uncontrollable individualist, iconoclast, unstable nonconformist." It's grown into an adjective ("he made a maverick decision") and become a verb (*mavericking, mavericked*).[3]

And yet, of all words that originated in the Old West and survived in common use to the present day, *maverick* is "the least understood and most corrupted." Its trajectory from the south Texas ranchlands into seemingly every aspect of modern life has made it "a word origin classic."[4]

Maverick is "a truly American word," notes the Voice of America's Learning English program. In a five-minute audio segment online, VOA's Anna Matteo, whose son's middle name is Maverick, explains the meaning as "a person who thinks independently" and "refuses to follow the customs or rules of a group to which he or she belongs." She gets the origin basically correct, enhanced with sound effects of cattle. Eiji Chiba in Japan responded with a post that in Japanese the word for a maverick is "ippiki-ookami," meaning "lone wolf." Marina in Ukraine wrote that a similar expression in her country is "white crow," a rare species that has to hide because of its light plumage.[5]

Poet Albert Huffstickler called *maverick* an "expansive word, as wide and deep as a west Texas sky at sunset, a word designed to continue expanding as people continue to alter the ways in which they manifest their variety and eccentricity. It's a democratic word. It refuses to leave anyone out, refuses to deny anyone the right to his basic uniqueness . . . a term designed to include and contain the unincludeable and . . . make them a part of things without ever infringing on their basic identity."[6]

But exactly what the word means still seems to be such a mystery that Merriam-Webster lists *maverick* in the top 10 percent of its most-looked-up words. To start piecing things together, we begin with Sam Maverick himself.[7]

TWO

Sam, the Original Maverick

Widespread fascination with cowboys and sheriffs and wide-open spaces made Texas ground zero for frontier tales and legends. Mythmakers and tale-tellers had free rein over the story of Sam Maverick, with no thorough biography to refute them for more than a century after his death. Fables leapfrogged each other until Sam Maverick became not only the biggest cattle owner in the country but also the biggest landowner in all the world except for the czar of Russia.

If he briefly owned only a few cattle, Sam Maverick did ultimately own more than three hundred thousand acres, scattered across thirty-two counties in central and western Texas. But that was scarcely 2 percent of all the land in Texas, and others had more. Outgoing south Texas rancher Richard King owned twice as much land by the time he died, fifteen years after Sam Maverick, assembled with fewer purchases and most of it in one contiguous, legendary ranch.

But Maverick's more reserved manner left people to guess what his long-term multiple land purchases were coming to, building a sense of mystery that snowballed speculations into myths that at the time could exceed even those of actual mega-ranchers like King.[1]

Having the obligatory Texas association with land and cattle, however exaggerated, Sam Maverick myths were enhanced by knowledge of his association with Alamo martyrs and other Texas pioneer icons, by his having dealt with Indians, and by hardships he endured after being seized by invading Mexican soldiers and marched as a prisoner deep into Mexico. Nor was he known to shrink from hardship. On one fraught wilderness expedition he joined, the men were reduced to dealing with "great thirst" by chewing the tops of their leather boots.[2]

Sam Maverick did not come into clear focus until the 1980s, when biographer Paula Mitchell Marks dug through the detritus and the mountains of original materials to at last produce a balanced, cohesive portrayal of Sam Maverick. At the same time she fleshed out a parallel portrait of his wife, Mary Adams Maverick, one of the notable women of the Texas frontier.

But by then the genie was long out of the bottle, and it was still tempting for historians, writers, and others to keep picking their favorites from the familiar smorgasbord of Maverick yarns, even as the question arose as to whether Sam Maverick was a maverick at all.

This line of thinking goes that Sam Maverick worked as "a prudent, rational lawyer" within the traditional social and political system, achieved wealth through careful and steady investments in land, and was such an accepted member of the establishment that he was repeatedly elected to high public office, in which he performed consistently and responsibly. Though living in a frontier town connected with the rest of the world only by long, rutted roads, he and his wife sent five sons to college in the East and in Europe.[3]

On the other hand, though he may have not fit the image of a raging nonconformist, he can nonetheless be seen as a maverick in his independent behavior. A wanderer, he thrived on the hardships of strenuous adventure far from civilization and disdained traditional trappings of wealth. He rejected the southern plantation culture he and his wife were raised in and opposed popular secessionist views up to the brink of the Civil War.[4]

Sam Maverick would have felt at home dealing with issues of the early twenty-first century. He supported Spanish-speaking Tejanos and sought to have state documents printed in Spanish as well as English. He opposed Know-Nothings' efforts to strip undocumented immigrants of their rights and to exclude San Antonio's Hispanic Catholics from government: "These Catholics threw in their share with the others and they bought this country, and I find that they like it, and I am happy to see it." In a letter to the editor in 1855 he wrote that America's gates "are open to all the world, and who would shut them." The continent was to become a "field for the regeneration of all mankind," where immigrants could "come and learn that men are still friends, though they do not think alike."[5]

He encouraged humane treatment of blacks (though he participated in the slavery system), agreed with "that fine old Quaker" Lucretia Mott and other early woman suffragists he once heard at a program in New York, and, unlike so many husbands of the time, trusted his wife's ability to help with decisions.[6]

Long before there were income taxes and deductions to encourage charitable contributions, Sam Maverick shared his wealth. His donations included land for San Antonio's Travis Park and for a station on the long-sought railroad, which finally reached the city seven years after his death in 1870.[7]

South Carolina patriarch Samuel Maverick's portrait is attributed to Samuel F. B. Morse.

Woven through all this are clues that explain his much-debated role in the cattle business, a venture that ultimately gave him prominence out of all proportion to his other accomplishments.

Sam Maverick's story starts in 1803 with his patrician birth in South Carolina, which assured him ease in dealing with both his father's business interests in the coastal port of Charleston and with the more sedate pace of plantation life in upcountry Pendleton, his birthplace some two hundred miles northwest.

Samuel Augustus Maverick was known to his family as Gus and to everyone else as Sam. He was nine at the time of the death of his maternal grandfather, Robert Anderson, called "Old Thunder Gusty" by the Cherokees, a brigadier general who served in the Revolutionary War and namesake of the nearby city of Anderson and its county. Parallels in their frontier activities are "striking," for the grandson also surveyed and bought land on a new frontier and, notes Paula Marks, likewise served Texas "in the same capacities in which his grandfather served South Carolina."[8]

Sam also had a role model in his father, Samuel, who so prospered in the import business that by the age of thirty he had already rebuilt the family fortune lost during the American Revolution. The family moved permanently from Charleston to the Pendleton countryside when Sam was seven. He went off to graduate from Yale in 1825 and three years later left for Winchester, Virginia, where he studied at the proprietary law school run by the noted jurist Henry St. George Tucker. He returned to hang out his shingle in Pendleton, then the most important town in that corner of South Carolina.

Still picturesque today, the perimeter of Pendleton's broad central green is sprinkled with vintage shops and offices. On the green you can sit down to lunch with a chilled sugar snap pea soup, follow that with farfalle rustica, and end with a pairing of rich chocolate ganache cake and a half-pour of Schlinkhaus Dorfelder sweet red wine. You'd be dining at 1826 Bistro on the Green. Its outdoor tables spill onto a patio past the four Doric columns fronting a two-story gleaming white Greek Revival jewel box dropped into the center of the green in 1826. It was once Farmers Society Hall, a lodge for the elite group of planters who elected Sam Maverick a member when he came home from Yale.

Beyond, the two-lane Old Greenville Highway weaves northeast from Pendleton through rolling wooded hills and fields for three miles before reaching Montpelier. The 1849 frame home was set back on a knoll by Sam's father, patriarch

South Carolina patriarch Samuel Maverick built a new Montpelier in 1849 to replace the burned earlier plantation home nearby.

Samuel Maverick, to replace the burned family plantation home on the crest of a low hill across the way. Mavericks have long since departed. Its commanding feature remains a classic portico supported by four two-story square wooden columns.

A half-mile beyond is the family cemetery, up a rise of the field to the east. Samuel Maverick's and a half dozen other graves are tightly wrapped within a chain-link fence topped by barbed wire. They look out over the smattering of ranch-style homes across the countryside. Below, a mile down State Road 39-18 toward Eighteenmile Creek, luminescent green state signs mark the structure over Highway 123 as Samuel Maverick Bridge.[9]

At the edge of Pendleton near the turn toward Montpelier is the white clapboard St. Paul's Episcopal Church, finished in 1822. Parishioners once included the Mavericks and John C.

Calhoun, whose restored home, some three miles northwest, is a centerpiece of the campus of Clemson University. When Sam Maverick returned to Pendleton to practice law, Calhoun was serving as vice president under John Quincy Adams and would continue under Andrew Jackson. Calhoun was a fervent advocate for slavery and the right of southern states to nullify the federal tariffs he believed unfairly favored northern states. His rigid views along with his square jaw, piercing eyes, and angry mop of graying hair earned him the nickname "cast-iron man." Most neighbors around Pendleton agreed with him.

But Calhoun's position rankled the Mavericks, father and son.

There was no way a state should have the right to nullify federal action, they believed. When his father was heckled for opposing nullification at a public meeting, a family story goes, Sam challenged the heckler to a duel, wounded him, then nursed him back to health. As the story grew, the identity of Sam's putative adversary became Calhoun himself, a legend Yale perpetuates in Maverick's university biography.[10]

The issue drew out Sam's inner maverick. He got riled enough to oppose nullification in a run for the South Carolina legislature in 1830, condemning the "cup of delusion" Calhoun and others were offering. Among thirteen candidates, Maverick finished ninth. But civility prevailed. The next year he was helping host a dinner in Calhoun's honor, and he remained sufficiently acceptable in the community to be chosen warden of St. Paul's.

Samuel Maverick, though, could see that his son, nearly thirty, was chafing at the limitations of Pendleton life. Politically he was out of step with the majority, and his law practice languished. Perhaps it would be a good idea for him to spend some time managing one of the family's numerous properties elsewhere.

So the patriarch gave his son a plantation along the Natchez Trace near Florence in northwestern Alabama. As he left Pendleton, Sam took with him twenty horses along with a wagon, a carriage, today's equivalent of nearly $20,000 in cash, and forty-five slaves. He may have been uneasy about slavery, but, writes his biographer, "he nonetheless remained a product of his culture, an antebellum slaveholder tacitly accepting and participating in the slave system until its demise."[11]

But Sam Maverick, restless, did not like being tied down at a plantation and was anxious to get out and start his own land empire. On a business trip to New Orleans he heard of opportunities in Mexican territory to the west. On March 16, 1835, only two months after leaving Pendleton, Sam Maverick bolted for Texas.

At New Orleans he boarded a ship that took him to Velasco—today's Freeport—at the mouth of the Brazos River in Texas, forty miles down the coast from Galveston and sixty miles due south of present-day Houston. Texas, part of Mexico's Province of Coahuila and Texas, was thinly populated by some thirty thousand residents, eight thousand of them Anglo-Americans settled legally in Texas during the previous decade and a half. Most lived within the arc roughly formed by its Spanish-era communities, Nacogdoches at the northeast, San Antonio at the west, and La Bahía/Goliad at the south.

Ominously, the Anglo-Americans were troubled by losing

freedoms promised under the 1824 constitution. Restoring them would make many protesters content to remain under Mexican rule, but newer and unsanctioned arrivals from the east were demanding outright independence or annexation by the United States.

In a month, Sam Maverick made his first Texas land purchase, more than a thousand acres on Lavaca Bay, one hundred miles down the coast from Velasco, bought with a friend made while taking a steamboat up the Brazos River. He spent most of the summer scouting lands in the Brazos region, ignoring mounting political tensions. In September he ventured to San Antonio, a few days' ride to the west.[12]

A month later Sam Maverick found himself under house arrest. A Mexican soldier stood guard at the door.

San Antonio was about as far west as you could get north of the Rio Grande and still find a semblance of civilization. The peculiar-looking town was established by Spain in 1718 as an outpost between the meddlesome French on the Louisiana border and vulnerable Spanish silver mines in northern Mexico. Its narrow streets were supposed to grow in an orderly grid from two central plazas. Instead, many streets stretched every which way as they followed acequias, the winding ditches that coaxed drinking and irrigation water downhill from the narrow San Antonio River that rose from springs two miles north.

Siestas gave a break from the afternoon heat. Cowboys enjoyed horse races and cockfights. There were religious processions, frequent gunfights, and, now and then, a hanging. At night came fandangos—candlelit Spanish dances to guitars and violins, castanets and clapping—mixed with generous shots of whiskey.

Sam Maverick arrived in San Antonio on September 8, 1835, and immediately fell in love with the place. "Something in him responded strongly to the pleasantly foreign antiquity of its Spanish churches and homes, to the great sweep of prairie to the west as well as to the gradually rising slopes to the north," writes his biographer. "The lands beyond were to be his joy, his solace and his passion."[13]

San Antonio was the most important town in Texas and once the provincial capital. But its population was shrinking from two thousand to eight hundred in the face of political turmoil that would cause its national government to change five times in less than fifty years. Violence and brutality could be medieval. Spanish soldiers once hung the head of a rebellious presidio commander from a pole in the center of Military Plaza.

Sam Maverick secured lodging with John W. Smith, who had married a Mexican citizen and was in the midst of land deals. Maverick made his own first land purchase in San Antonio fifteen days after he arrived and bought a second tract two days later.[14]

But Maverick's landlord was disillusioned with the Mexican government, and rebellion was approaching. The next month the brother-in-law of Mexican dictator Santa Anna, General Martín Perfecto de Cos, showed up with an army of seven hundred to hold San Antonio and the nearby Alamo mission. He placed a guard at Smith's house, forbidding Smith and Maverick from leaving the city.

For his military service in San Antonio in 1835, Sam Maverick received this land certificate from the Republic of Texas for 640 acres. He redeemed it in 1851 for a tract near the Rio Grande.

Cos, however, soon found San Antonio surrounded and put under siege by four hundred Texians, as Texans were called prior to annexation by the United States. On December 1, Cos inexplicably freed both Smith and Maverick, who crossed the lines to help galvanize the fractious Texian army into action. Three days later Kentuckian Ben Milam—guided by Sam Maverick—and a firebrand named Francis W. Johnson led a two-pronged attack into San Antonio. Then came five days of door-to-door combat.

Today, near a floodgate where the San Antonio River turns sharply past a Holiday Inn to enter the Great Bend, a QR code tops a short post along the River Walk. It marks the towering cypress—now ninety feet tall, its canopy as wide—climbed by a Mexican sniper on December 7, 1835. Taking aim across the river down into a courtyard teeming with Texian soldiers, the sniper felled Ben Milam, who died in Sam Maverick's arms.

The Texians, however, won. General Cos surrendered and retreated to Mexico, promising his troops would never return. But his furious brother-in-law, Antonio López de Santa Anna, president of Mexico, vowed to stamp out the rebellious Texians for good.

The grassy plains of south Texas did not lend themselves to military defense. But along the river within ten miles of San Antonio, high stone walls surrounded five abandoned Spanish mission complexes. Armies at one time or another took refuge within four of them. The most strategically located old mission, known as the Alamo, stood on a bluff across the river from town.

Sam Maverick stayed in San Antonio, buying tracts of land up to a week before Santa Anna appeared. He and other Texas partisans in San Antonio intended to fortify themselves inside the Alamo if necessary while other Texians were planning a convention at their capital, Washington-on-the-Brazos, to declare independence and write a constitution for a Republic of Texas. Longtime Mexican-Texian partisans in San Antonio, sensing Anglo-Americans in their midst as transients, elected only four of their own to represent San Antonio at the convention. Those at the Alamo garrison thought they should be heard as well. They chose as delegates two lawyers from South Carolina, James Bonham and Sam Maverick. Both had begun practices in Pendleton the same year, though they were on opposite sides of the states' rights issue. But Bonham "preferred action to deliberation" and declined his election.[15]

Louisianan Jesse Badgett, chosen in Bonham's place, left for the convention in mid-February. Maverick lingered until March 2, barely missing Santa Anna's siege. John W. Smith departed shortly after with a last desperate plea for reinforcements. Four days later, as Maverick signed the Texas Declaration of Independence, all Alamo defenders had been killed, though the news did not reach the convention for a week. Sam Houston rallied Texians at San Jacinto, near the future city of Houston, surprised Santa Anna on April 21, and won independence for the new republic.

But Sam Maverick had fallen ill at the convention. It took him three weeks to recover. In the interlude he worried about his abrupt departure from the United States and his year-long neglect of family duties. Guilty though he felt for having survived the Alamo massacre and leaving the Texas War of Independence, he set his inner maverick aside and headed back to Alabama and South Carolina to help pull things back together.[16]

THREE

True Grit

Sam Maverick, thirty-three, was on his way back from Texas in May 1836 when, near Tuscaloosa, Alabama, he greeted another lone rider, Mary Ann Adams, eighteen. They dismounted. Sam saw she was as tall as he—six feet—and he could look her straight in the eye. They were married three months later. After his death, she found in his effects a snippet of the green muslin dress she was wearing the day they met.

For a year the newlyweds stayed at Pendleton, where their first child, Samuel, was born. But the pull of Texas was irresistible, and in December 1837 the young family headed for San Antonio. With them were seven slaves; one, Jack, age eight, was destined to play an unknowing but critical role in the growth of the English lexicon.

After a stop at Mary Adams Maverick's plantation home at Tuscaloosa, the party grew to fourteen. They traveled with a carriage, three extra saddle horses, and a Kentucky wagon packed with a tent, bedding, and provisions, with space left for the cook and children. Around New Year's Day 1838 they crossed from Louisiana into Texas.

What was to come in the turbulent run-up to the word *maverick* lays bare the true grit of pioneers who tamed the West. For soon, wrote Sam Maverick's wife, came "a dreadful time."

"About January 26 we entered a bleak, desolate swamp-prairie cut up by what were called dry bayous, i.e., deep gullies, now almost full of water," Mary Maverick recalled in her *Memoirs*, considered the first autobiography written in Texas. "We had passed Mr. Bridge's, the last house before we got into this dreadful prairie, and had to cross the Navidad before we got to Mr. Keer's, the next habitation. Every step of the animals was in water, sometimes knee-deep. We stalled in five or six gullies. Each time the wagon had to be unloaded in water, rain and north wind, and all the men and animals had to work together to pull us out."[1]

"The first norther I ever experienced struck us here," she added. "This was a terrific howling north wind with a fine rain, blowing and penetrating through clothes and blankets. Never in my life had I felt such cold." Nevertheless she could look back on the ordeal as "a delightful trip all through, with the exception of [the] four days' journey across a prairie swamp and one night's adventure with Indians."[2]

About two-thirds of the way from the Texas border to San Antonio, Sam Maverick set up the group to board with an acquaintance on the Navidad River and rode ahead to assess San Antonio's safety for his family. He found the town "putting on a neglected & ruinous appearance" but still "strikingly pretty and oriental in its look." Four months later, with more land purchased, he rejoined his family for the two-week trek to San Antonio.[3]

Repairing a broken wagon wheel one afternoon was among the lesser hurdles of getting through the sparsely settled countryside. Once the wheel was fixed and the travelers began breaking camp came a greater challenge. Seventeen well-armed

William Samuel's 1849 portrayal of the east side of Main Plaza shows the Maverick home at the upper left, below a cypress tree growing up from the banks of the San Antonio River.

Tonkawas appeared, still in war paint from a battle with Comanches, and displayed two scalps. "I was frightened almost to death," Mary Maverick wrote, "but tried not to show my alarm.

"They rode up to the carriage window and asked to see the papoose. First one, then another came. I held up my little Sammy and smiled at their compliments. But I took care to have my pistol and bowie knife visible and kept cool, and declined most decidedly when they asked me to hand the baby out to them that they might 'see how pretty and white he was.'"[4]

As the Mavericks started out, the Tonkawas rode beside them. But the Mavericks' entourage included six fully armed men. This discouraged the Tonkawas sufficiently that by dawn only two of them remained.

The Mavericks arrived in San Antonio in mid-June 1838.

The next few years accelerated at the pace of a western thriller. They enlarged their three-room stone house at the northeast corner of Main Plaza, in the shade of a cypress rising from the river below, where they built a bathhouse in the water. There were constant dangers. During the first summer, Comanches twice raided the town at night, killing three residents and kidnapping a child.

A few doors down, in March 1840, Comanche chieftains were negotiating in the locked council house over the return of white hostages when things went very wrong. Reported Mary Maverick: "The Comanches instantly, with one accord, raised a terrific war whoop, drew their arrows and commenced firing with deadly effect, at the same time making efforts to break out of the hall." The county judge, the sheriff, and five other Texians lay dead.[5]

As the melee spilled outside, bystanders scattered. Two Comanches passed Mary Maverick while she ran toward her house. As she ducked inside, one followed her to the door. "He turned to raise his hand to push it just as I beat down the heavy bar." That Comanche ran on, but three others got through the side gate trying for the river. Jinny, the slave cook from Pendleton, children clustered around her, grabbed a large rock and threatened the trio off. Pursuers shot two of the Comanches as the third broke away.[6]

When it was over, thirty-three Comanches were dead and the surviving thirty-two were prisoners.

A Russian naturalist and surgeon remembered only as Dr. Weideman gathered four Comanche cadavers to preserve the skeletons as specimens. At night he put them in a soap boiler, saved the bones, and emptied the rest into the acequia that passed his home. The next day, Mary Maverick recalled, "it dawned upon the dwellers upon the banks of the ditch that the doctor had defiled their drinking water. There arose a great hue and cry." Arrested and brought to trial, Dr. Weideman took the abuse heaped upon him "quite calmly," assured citizens that the residue had run off long before daybreak, "paid his fine and went off, laughing."[7]

To help deal with expected Comanche retaliation, Sam Maverick was one of the minutemen who kept horses at the ready to respond to any alarm sounded by the bell of the Church of San Fernando. But even during the council house affray his wife felt little fear, explaining, "I was just twenty-two then, and was endowed with a fair share of curiosity."[8]

Sam, by then the father of three, was elected mayor and later to the congress of the struggling republic. He practiced law, argued cases in court, and continued surveying and buying land, as he and his father back in South Carolina believed that when things settled down there would be a rush of land-seeking settlers from the United States. The patriarch sent funds to purchase land in trust for his grandchildren. By 1840 Sam Maverick owned 4,600 acres. Nearly half was a tract he was particularly optimistic about, at Cox's Point just up from Matagorda Bay across from present-day Port Lavaca, "which I consider a site for a future city."[9]

Frightening though Indian raids may have been, armies moving up from Mexico were another matter. Santa Anna could not reconcile himself to the surrender he had signed at San Jacinto. In and out as Mexico's president, by 1842 he was in again and determined to strike back. Soon San Antonians learned that Mexican troops were on the way. On March 1 the

Mavericks and their neighbors fled east on horseback. Two days later word arrived that San Antonio had fallen. Sam Maverick and others went back to join three hundred men and retake the town, but the Mexicans left without a fight.

With San Antonio no longer a safe place, Maverick purchased twenty-six acres near La Grange, a hundred miles east of San Antonio, and set up his family in a log home. He went back to check on his plantation in Alabama and returned to La Grange then to go on, alone, to San Antonio.

On September 5, 1842, Sam Maverick was in court defending a client over an unpaid municipal fee when warning came that an unknown force was close to town. Those in the courtroom fled to Maverick's nearby home. The invaders turned out to be as many as 1,800 Mexican soldiers under Gen. Adrian Woll. Fifty-three Texians, including Sam Maverick, were seized as prisoners of war. All were respected citizens, two of them—Maverick and William E. Jones—sitting members of the Congress of the Republic of Texas.

Sam Maverick got word to his wife: "I will not now mourn over what could not be avoided." She sent a slave, Griffin, to join a company led by Capt. Nicholas Dawson on its way to retake San Antonio. Griffin was to pose as a runaway but carry ransom money if needed to free his master. Near town they were surprised by Mexican cavalry. Thirty-five Texians, including Griffin, were killed in what became known as the Dawson Massacre.

Already Sam Maverick and his fellow captives were crossing the Rio Grande. Their 2,000-mile march ended three months later in chains in the gloomy eighteenth-century moated fortress known as Perote Prison. They were joined by another storied group of captured Texians, seized during the Mier Expedition that had tried to take Santa Fe, New Mexico. Those prisoners escaped on the march down. But 176 were recaptured, and, once ensconced at Perote, every tenth man was to be shot. All drew from a jar containing 176 beans, seventeen of them black. Those drawing black ones were executed. As he watched others draw, William "Bigfoot" Wallace, who became a legendary Texas Ranger, observed that the black beans were larger than the white ones. He successfully fingered a white bean and survived.

Although Sam Maverick wrote of camping on the trek down "in cow dung a foot thick" and of overnighting in places "which appeared to be used as a privy," he maintained his adventurous spirit and equanimity and seemed almost to enjoy the exertion along the way. His biographer thought his journal entries of those days could be mixed with those in his 1835 land-surveying journal "without the reader's noticing a significant difference in tone." Despite the privations of Perote, prisoners were able to slip out letters and, on rare occasions, to receive them. Sam Maverick lamented to his wife the loss of Griffin: "God knows I feel his death as the hardest piece of fortune we have suffered in Texas . . . a true and faithful friend and a brother, a worthy dear brother in arms."[10]

He also got out a plea for help to Waddy Thompson, a former South Carolina congressman married to one of Sam Maverick's cousins; Thompson happened to be U.S. minister to Mexico. He got the letter shortly after receiving a similar request from Sam Maverick's father. As a favor, Thompson began working on the release of all Texians. Santa Anna first freed the two Texas congressmen—Maverick and William Jones—and the Western District's presiding judge, Anderson Hutchinson. In April 1843 the three boarded an American naval ship one hundred miles east at Vera Cruz and headed home. Maverick took with him a ten-link section of the chain that had bound him and his drinking gourd; both ended up in museum collections. The last of the prisoners were freed by the fall of 1844.

Sam Maverick rejoined his family near La Grange. He sold his Alabama plantation to finance further land deals. On a trip back east, he expressed annoyance at the ignorance of friends and even family members about Texas. In Charleston, he complained to his wife, "wits and wiseacres have not yet discerned any difference between Matamoras and Matagorda. An old school fellow last night wanted me to give him a very particular account of the 'narrow place across' to the Pacific, meaning Panama, which he supposed in Texas."[11]

As the family stayed near La Grange, tensions with Mexico showed no sign of abating, and San Antonio was still not a safe place for a family. While returning from New Orleans, Sam Maverick stopped on the Gulf of Mexico at the mouth of Matagorda Bay close to his first Texas land purchase, nine years earlier. There he sensed a climate, community, and safety better than at La Grange. In mid-November 1844 the family began its move south to Matagorda Peninsula.

The distance was less than two hundred miles, but the journey took three full weeks. The caravan of one carriage, two wagons, a few saddle horses, and seven cows slogged along swampy roads through cold winds and rain. At night the family camped when the occasional lodging could not be found. On one particularly hard day the caravan was almost across the

For the middle half of the nineteenth century, cumbersome ox-drawn wagons were the main transport for commercial and household goods from the Texas coast inland through south Texas and San Antonio, which lacked rail access until 1877.

last of three sloughs when a wagon stalled and one of its oxen fell. The men pried the ox out of the mud and double-teamed the wagon to get through. They made eight miles that day and camped, though "in the night it rained and a norther blew up, and we all got cold and wet."[12]

Finally, on December 7, 1844, they reached the tip of Matagorda Peninsula to stay with Alexander Somervell, a military leader who had been with Sam Maverick during the siege of San Antonio and was a customs collector living at DeCrow's Point.

FOUR

A Cattle Deal
with an ex-Pirate

Of the two well-known images of Samuel Augustus Maverick, the more familiar is the posthumous painting by Carl G. von Iwonski from a photograph. It shows a gentleman appearing older than his sixty-seven years, distinguished in a buttoned jacket and broad bow tie and reflectively gazing away from the viewer through dark, sensitive eyes. Long white locks are combed back from a high forehead and down either side of an oval face emphasized by a well-trimmed moustache drooping above a goatee.

A photograph taken perhaps twenty years earlier shows a Sam Maverick with whitening hair combed back but with a face clean-shaven. He looks directly out with a penetrating gaze and lips pursed as if awaiting a response. He wears a formal tie, but his jacket hangs impatiently open, perhaps ignored in thoughts of a dash to the next opportunity.

That would be the Sam Maverick of Matagorda Peninsula—erstwhile Alabama plantation owner, former Texas revolutionary and chained prisoner at Perote, once and future mayor of San Antonio and emerging land baron, then in virtual exile on a spit of land in the Gulf of Mexico until the course of the

The restless Sam Maverick of Matagorda Peninsula was looking for deals, including land, steamboats, and cattle.

Mexican War would make it safe to take his growing family back to San Antonio.

But for a restless fortysomething marking time at what must have seemed the far edge of the known world, there could still be plenty to do and many deals to be done.

Real estate opportunities begged to be seized. New towns were on the drawing boards for hordes of expected immigrants. Sam Maverick already owned nearly two thousand acres ready for subdividing at Cox's Point nearby. Now he bought a one-third interest in Thomas DeCrow's townsite at the tip of Matagorda Peninsula—DeCrow's Point, also known as Port Cavallo, where the channel named Cavallo Pass led into Matagorda Bay. Nor did Maverick ignore potential elsewhere. He made numerous trips back to beleaguered San Antonio, seat of then far-flung Bexar County, to make and register in its courthouse new deals that soon extended his scattered holdings to more than sixty-five thousand acres.[1]

There was a bright future for homebuilding. While on a five-month trip to South Carolina, Maverick stopped in Mobile, Alabama, to order a shipload of lumber to build homes in DeCrow's Point.[2]

There were steamboats. Navigation was foreseen up the Colorado River from Matagorda Bay even as far inland as Austin. Maverick bought a half interest in Thomas DeCrow's "little steamer," the *Delta*, on the Colorado. They got a state contract to dredge logs obstructing the river at its mouth.[3]

And, this being Texas, there were cattle.

Matagorda Peninsula, fifty-one miles long and never more than a mile wide, would have been a barrier island had it not been connected at its northeastern end to the Texas mainland. Its gentle arc of narrow sandy beach facing the gulf rises to a thin grassy plain before tapering down on the far side to a ragged coastline of inlets and estuaries along Matagorda Bay, helping form a natural harbor. Fierce hurricanes periodically sweeping off the gulf ultimately taught residents the futility of rebuilding, and the peninsula, doubly plagued with harsh heat in the summer, was eventually deserted. It was used for an army airfield and aerial gunnery/bombing range during World War II and later as a rocket launch site. Today the peninsula is virtually uninhabited, with a new ship channel cut across it to Port O'Connor and campsites at a 1,600-acre nature park. Its dunes and coastal marshes provide one of the nation's finest birding areas.

But to unknowing early arrivals the bay area seemed to

Mary A. Maverick, shown in the 1860s, thought Matagorda had "the most cultivated society in the state."

have rich prospects. From DeCrow's Point, southwest across the shallow natural channel leading into Matagorda Bay was Matagorda Island. On the northern shore of the bay at the mouth of the Colorado River, the town of Matagorda had a population of a thousand by 1844, with hotels, churches, theaters, and three schools along its mud streets. "At that time," thought Mary Maverick, "Matagorda had probably the most cultivated society in the state."[4]

Once his shipload of lumber arrived from Mobile, early in 1847, Maverick took some of it to build a three-story, eight-room home for his family at DeCrow's Point. It was most likely a raised cottage with a steep pitched roof in the style of early homes along the Gulf Coast to the north and east, positioned to catch the breeze and to avoid high water. It had a front outdoor stairway more than twelve feet up, likely rising above util-

Hotels, churches, theaters, and three schools lined the mud streets of the port of Matagorda, on the mainland side of Matagorda Bay.

ity rooms to two upper floors, safe from storm surges. While on the stairway working on the house, Sam Maverick tripped on a loose upper step, fell to the ground and was knocked unconscious. He sprained his shoulder and twisted his neck so he could not sit up or feed himself for more than a week. But he made a full recovery, and in April the family moved in.[5]

"The house was very substantially built and was calculated to resist a very considerable storm," wrote Mary Maverick. "It commanded a fine view of both the bay and the gulf." There was little on the peninsula to impede the view. "We never saw any trees during the three years we lived there," remembered son Samuel, "nothing but Spanish Dagger. I nearly forgot how trees looked."[6]

As Maverick was putting the finishing touches on the new house, there came an opportunity to diversify into the cattle business. In early February 1847 he struck a deal with Charles Nathan Tilton for a herd of cattle at a farm known as Tiltona twenty-one miles north, halfway up the peninsula. Tilton, forty-seven, had been born into a New Hampshire family with twelve children, left home to seek adventure, and ended up on

Sam Maverick bought his cattle in this agreement, signed in 1847 with Charles Tilton, a former pirate with Jean Lafitte.

shipboard as boatswain's mate with Jean Lafitte, the legendary pirate based on Galveston Island. In 1829, presumably having had his fill of adventure, Tilton settled down on a 102-acre farm on the bay side of Matagorda Peninsula, with its own inlet and an oyster bayou. He married and raised a family. He seems to have enlarged the farm, for its sale price of $500—$15,000 in today's dollars—at the contemporary price of land suggests a size of just under 500 acres.[7]

But the bigger part of the deal was the cattle, costing more than twice as much as the land. They were priced at three dollars a head for up to 450 head, with no charge for any beyond that number. A few oxen had the same price tag. Before the closing, Tilton was to brand any cattle not already branded. He agreed "to throw in without charge" any cattle beyond 450 along with "whatever hogs there may be, also an ox cart and ox yoke and all lumber, logs &c. lying about the premises." Said son Samuel, "I was told that the man went off with a bucket of silver."[8]

Jinny and her son Jack and three other slaves were sent up to run things. One family friend thought Jinny "the kindest and best" of all the slaves she had seen. Another saw her as "the most perfect lady on the Peninsula."[9]

The Maverick family left DeCrow's Point at least twice for spring and summer vacations at Tiltona, once overland by cart and horseback and later by boat. "We spent a delightful week drinking fresh milk, fishing, bathing in the breakers, riding and having a general good time," Mary Maverick remembered of one visit. They took home "chickens and turkeys, butter and eggs, fresh beef and other farm products," plus an abundance of figs.[10]

Back home on the tip of the peninsula, Samuel Jr., nine, and his brother Lewis, seven, helped tend the family's four-acre garden, raising "wonderful quantities of vegetables, sweet potatoes, watermelons." Soldiers disembarking at DeCrow's Point on their way to or from the Mexican War got word of the fresh melons. The men happily gathered them and, recalled Sam Jr., "handed me so many nickels, dimes and quarters that I thought I was the richest boy in the world." Along the shore the brothers gathered,

*Jinny, who came as a slave
from South Carolina to Texas
with the Mavericks, was the
mother of Jack—charged with
branding Sam Maverick's
cattle—and lived to be 106.*

sacked and sold coal washed up from shipwrecks, accumulated
$12 apiece—today's equivalent of $700—and bought two head
of cattle and some calves to enlarge the family herd.[11]

With a new house, a productive farm and cattle operation
within range, and diversions in the bay's ports of Matagorda,
Lavaca, and Indianola, their circumstances seemed idyllic. But
San Antonio was beckoning them back. U.S. Army troops had
been stationed in San Antonio since the annexation of Texas to
the United States in 1845, bringing a permanent end to Indian
raids. Nor were invasions from Mexico a worry any longer as
the Mexican War was ending, winding up territorial disputes
at last. In mid-October 1847, eight months after buying Tiltona
and the cattle, the family returned.

Mary Maverick and the youngest children took the new
stagecoach from Lavaca to San Antonio. They arrived nine

days later to find "everything covered in dust and the heat dreadful," and their home on Main Plaza in great need of repair. Sam Jr. and the older ones packed the household goods into hired wagons and followed. A few slaves stayed at Tiltona. Jinny's son, Jack, nineteen, the only male, was placed in charge of the cattle.[12]

Sam Maverick's venture into the cattle business did not excite his father. The patriarch remembered that sixty years earlier his uncle had taken five hundred cattle in payment of a debt and driven them to graze at Pendleton. "Cattle like an army of men don't thrive," he wrote his son. "They can't be kept & fattened that way, the very smell of one another gives them disease."[13]

But by the time the warning arrived, Sam Maverick and his family were back in San Antonio.

FIVE

Texas Longhorns on the Loose

The trail that leads from Sam Maverick's unbranded stray cattle on the pastures of Matagorda Peninsula into virtually every dictionary of the English language and to common use around the globe seems more convoluted than any blazed by the most wily calf trying to avoid the branding iron.

Apologists who posited that Maverick really didn't want the cattle but just took them in settlement of a debt cannot get past why not only there is no record of such a debt but why an experienced investor who never wanted to be in the cattle business in the first place would take nearly ten years to get out of it.

The story gets complicated by slavery. To gloss over it would bury a true telling of how people dealing with the injustices of the time have influenced our lives in unexpected ways and, in this case, caused our vocabulary to be enriched.

Thousands of African American slave cowboys lived in eastern Texas and in Indian nations to the north before the Civil War. Many had served apprenticeships with trained cowboys. Jack, however, only happened to be with the Mavericks at DeCrow's Point when Sam Maverick bought Tiltona and the cattle, and he was the only male sent to take care of the place. He seems to have had little training and less supervision. In Tiltona's isolation, Jack and the others lived, as some have said, as "nominally slave but essentially free."[1]

Jack got his own place in history. When two UCLA col-
leagues came out with *The Negro Cowboys* in 1965, Jack led off
the chapter "Slaves on Horseback." The authors did not track
down his name, which they assumed would never be known.
Yet they acknowledged him as "one of the early Negro cowboys," particularly notable despite having allegedly been "ineffi-
cient, even lazy," for having "made his master famous."[2]

As a lawyer and real estate investor with no prior experience
in the cattle business, Sam Maverick may have been encouraged by the old saying that all it took to run cattle was having a
man with "a rope, nerve to use it and a branding iron."[3] Jack was
legally required to stay put and needed only room and board;
whatever losses caused by his inexperience could be more than
offset by the expense and bother of hiring itinerant ranch
hands, Maverick's thinking seems to have gone. The cattle
thus could be managed inexpensively, like land, and their value
would grow with new yearlings until the market was right to
sell the herd at a profit.

The earliest stock at Tiltona was likely descended from
English Bakewell longhorns, large and lean beef cattle with
downward curving horns. First brought to the New World
to Virginia in the mid-1700s, the breed was favored by settlers from Kentucky and the lower South who were making
their way to east Texas, where remnants of the first Spanish
cattle had disappeared during revolutions and Indian raids.
But the hardier and smaller Spanish criollos, with their wider,
upturned horns, were returning by the 1840s, moving up
from the onetime Mexican ranches beyond the Nueces River.
Ranchers cross-breeding to better cope with harsh Texas
weather created the storied Texas longhorns—skinny, tough,

As they aged, Texas longhorns could grow horns with a spread of more than nine feet.

feral animals much different from the more beefy longhorns we know today.[4]

Texas longhorns were well adapted to south Texas. They developed immunity to deadly tick fever, produced calves over longer periods than other breeds, and fiercely protected their young by using their broad horns to toss or spear attacking predators like wolves and coyotes. Having long legs and hard hooves, they could range widely for water and grass. Self-sufficient, they thrived on marginal pastures, like the coarse grasses rimming the Gulf Coast and the sandy dunes of Matagorda Peninsula. With yet no fences to confine them, they were free to roam onto unused rangeland owned by other ranchers. This established legal range rights transferable with sale of the cattle, enabling small farms like Tiltona to be the base for large herds beyond the capacity of their limited acreage.[5]

Yearlings, however, needed to be branded to identify their ownership on the unfenced range. That process was a weak link in Sam Maverick's low-budget business plan.

Nursing calves were the property of whomever owned the mother. If not branded by their owner as soon as they were weaned, calves were legally owned by no one and were free to be branded by the first cowboy with an iron, regardless of whose land they were on. Spaniards brought that custom to New Spain, and through the nineteenth century wild and unbranded cattle in the American West were still considered public property.[6]

Many Texas counties began requiring brand registration, though not all ranchers complied. In 1837 Thomas DeCrow and a brother registered the sixth brand in Matagorda County. Charles Tilton and his wife, Anna, registered their separate brands in 1843. When Sam Maverick purchased Tiltona four years later, one requirement was that Tilton bring all branding of his cattle up to date. Sam Maverick first improvised on Charles Tilton's brand, combining PL—initials of the original owner, Philip Love—by extending lines of his own. Then he came up with a brand based on his own initials, SAM, a design more difficult for rustlers to alter. But it was used infrequently, if at all.[7]

The branding ritual was fundamental to successful ranching and required skill and good timing. Irons had to be heated in a wood fire and stamped quickly, burning through the animal's hair but not deeply into the skin, which could cause a sore to develop. Each stamp iron bore a rancher's distinctive logo, so ownership of an animal could be determined quickly

Sam Maverick devised a cattle brand using his initials, but it was used little, if ever.

when mixed with others on the open range. But rustlers could modify an imprint by using a "running iron" with a hooked tip to stamp on some portion of an existing brand and change its design, transferring title of the animal to the owner of the altered brand. Being caught with a running iron could result in a quick hanging.

Although it was a serious crime, even the most elaborate brands could be overburned and changed. The Texas Panhandle's XIT Ranch, one of the world's largest at more than three million acres, had a brand originally thought to be rustler-proof. The letters XIT were formed by one straight branding bar about five inches long being applied five times. Hasty work, however, could cause some of the five impressions to be slightly off kilter. Rustlers figured how to extend misapplied lines into a five-pointed star with a cross in the center, cancelling the XIT's mark of ownership. The solution became "the most widely told legend of brand burning in the Southwest.... Around their fires at night, or as they sit in the shade of a corral fence by day, someone will tell the story, and others, tracing the XIT in the sand between their bowlegs, will attempt to convert it into a Texas star with a cross in the center."[8]

Branding was not for the faint of heart and could go awry. Onetime rancher Anson Mills described how one attempt did:

The largest cattle were usually driven through a chute, and as they passed through the iron would be placed against them. This is an easier method than to throw the animal; the latter method is hard on the horse as well as the man. If the animal is thrown, however, the branding is usually a better job.

To throw an animal, one of the men roped it around the horns, another man by the hind legs, this latter being known as "heeling." The ropers then pulled in opposite directions, which straightened out the animal. Another man seized it by the tail and pulled it over on its side, when the brand was applied.

Some very laughable things occur during this work. The writer was responsible for one which was extremely funny for the audience but not for the victim.

I was obliged to rebrand some of my cattle. I went down to the butcher corral while my men were at work (at least, supposed to be), but when I arrived they were all sitting on the fence. I told them I was not paying them to hold down the fence boards. They told me a mad cow had driven them out of the corral. I laughed and said, "Let me have a rope and I'll show you how to do it; there is no danger."

There were two or more snubbing-posts in the corral. The cow was frothing at the mouth, pawing and acting in a fighting mood. My idea was to rope the cow and if she came for me I would jump behind one of the posts or climb the fence. It was a high board fence and rather hard to get over.

Taking the rope, I entered the corral, made a cast and by good luck roped her around the horns the first throw. Before I could pass the rope around the snubbing post, however, she came for me full speed, "head down and tail a rising!" There was a hog pen

Cowboys as young as Jack, who was in his early twenties when he was in charge of Sam Maverick's cattle, could manage branding through pens and chutes but needed help.

in one corner of the corral, and I made for that. I didn't pause to put my hand on the fence but took a header over the top board, landing in a mess of filth. When I staggered to my feet I was a sight! Luckily, no bones were broken.

The men were laughing fit to kill. They afterward told me that while I was in the air the cow struck the fence full tilt. The laugh was on me, and I had to go to the house and change my clothes. I sent the men a keg of beer, and didn't go to the corral again that day.[9]

Some ranches along the lower Brazos River a few dozen miles from Matagorda Bay ran two thousand or more cattle. They required large numbers of cowboys, who needed extra help from neighboring ranchers for roundups and brandings each spring. But a lone farmer could manage a small herd. One was encountered about this time by traveler Frederick Law Olmsted. "For about a month in the year he had to work hard," Olmsted wrote, "driving his cattle into the pen and roping and marking the calves; this was always done in a kind of frolic in the spring, the neighboring herdsmen assisting each other. During the rest of the year he hadn't anything to do. When he felt like it he got on to a horse and rode around and looked after his cattle; but that wasn't work, he said, 'twas only play."[10]

One cattleman, R. H. Williams, who ranched on the Frio River west of San Antonio, stressed, though, that "hunting of cows and calves, where cattle ranged over miles of country, was no child's play," for "the cows, half wild, with the instincts of their race, hid their calves in the chaparral, where it is hard to find them. But they had to be found, for the success in ranching depends on the careful and thorough manner in which calf hunting is done."[11]

Important though keeping close tabs on his cattle may have been, seven months after leaving Matagorda Peninsula Sam Maverick was sidelined by tragedy. In May 1847 he returned from a monthlong surveying trip to learn that his favorite daughter, Agatha, seven, had died after a weeklong illness. "She has wandered off in the dark and we will never more on Earth be able to find her," he mourned. As his grieving continued, his family knew he needed an extreme distraction to recover.[12]

The sort of adventure that always seemed to rejuvenate him materialized the next year in the form of an expedition funded by local businessmen to go into unexplored, rugged regions of west Texas and find a suitable trade route from San Antonio to El Paso, now covered by Interstate 10 in 550 miles. The effort was funded by Sam Antonio businessmen and was to be led by Maverick's friend and legendary Texas Ranger Jack Hays.

Thirty-five men, including Sam Maverick, headed west in August 1848. They little anticipated how soon they would be "scrambling along seemingly endless rock ledges and suffering a thousand torments of heat and thirst." Many promising trails proved impassable. Indians stole some of their horses and pack mules. When food was gone they ate bear grass, cactus tunas, and mules ("mule meat very poor and tough," Maverick noted) when not lucky enough to find and kill a panther, as they once did near the Rio Grande. At one point they fought thirst by chewing leather from their boots.[13]

After four months, the men gave up and returned. They had found several ways not to go. This helped an Army engineering expedition find a satisfactory route to El Paso the next year.

The trek did in fact renew Sam Maverick's health and his spirits. His wife quoted Jack Hays as calling Maverick "the most enduring and least complaining man of the party." Maverick's interests snapped back to business affairs. Before he left on the ill-fated El Paso expedition he heard from his sister-in-law Elizabeth Adams Clow, who was married to a merchant in Lavaca, that his cattle at Tiltona were "starving for grass and water." Now, in January 1849, he got in touch with Thomas DeCrow about selling their co-owned steamboat ("dead capital") and considered a trip to Tiltona to sell his cattle or to move them to his property nearer San Antonio on Cibolo Creek, "as they will not prosper on their present grass."[14]

But Maverick did not take the trip, and Jack was finding his job too difficult. The narrowness of Matagorda Peninsula did help confine cattle despite the lack of fences and might have enabled an older and better-trained cowhand to manage things, with seasonal help from a neighboring cowboy or two. But Jack was not getting help from nearby ranchers.

In November 1849, two years after the Mavericks left DeCrow's Point, Jack, most likely illiterate, recruited one John Graham to write Maverick on his behalf that "without assistance he finds it quite impossible to pen and brand your cattle on the Peninsula, and the stock is consequently becoming more wild and unmanageable daily."[15]

But Maverick, preoccupied with family matters, offered no aid. His household was fighting off cholera and influenza. His surviving daughter, Augusta, six, died. After that, the family began planning a more comfortable home, away from noisy Main Plaza, at the northwest corner of Alamo Plaza. As time passed, Jack seems to have given up on tending the cattle. His mother could do nothing with him. In February 1852 Mary Maverick got a report from her friend Maggie Pearson, wife of the doctor in Matagorda, that Jinny had not seen Jack for six months, and last heard of him being "over on some boat in the bay." During the winter many of the Maverick cattle had died, Maggie Pearson added, and Tiltona had gone "sadly out of repair."[16]

The Mavericks offered the Pearsons summertime use of Tiltona in exchange for making repairs, and the Pearsons were happy to accept. But the condition of the cattle did not improve. Jack later said that the young cattle were being stolen by cowboys who threatened to kill him if they found him on the range, so he had gone to work hauling watermelons for twenty dollars a month.[17]

Word got around that Maverick's cattle were being "lost or stolen from want of proper attention." Neighboring cattlemen, who began identifying unbranded cattle as Maverick's, were convinced that such an otherwise fastidious businessman and respected public figure must have lost interest in the cattle business and would be ready to sell. He began getting a stream of offers. His initial host at DeCrow's Point, Alexander Somervell, offered nearly four thousand acres on the Lavaca River for the cattle. One writer heard that Maverick was selling out and asked what the terms might be, as the cattle "have been awfully neglected, not branded ever since you left and will do you very little good situated as they are." Two cattlemen in eastern Matagorda County separately proposed swapping the cattle for land.[18]

In 1851 Solomon G. Cunningham, who two years earlier became a major shipper of live cattle from nearby Indianola to New Orleans, offered Maverick $10 a head in cash "for such as suit my trade," $4 per head for yearlings, and $2.50 each for good calves. Cunningham offered to pick them up at DeCrow's Point, but, as in the case with the other offers, there is no record of a response.[19]

In May 1853 an anonymous "friend to Justice," hearing that Maverick was out of the state, wrote Mary Maverick. Thinking that she may not have heard of the situation, and citing three others who had written her husband on the subject, in an uneven hand he advised her to "send someone to look after your stock of cattle immediately or you will not have in eighteen months from this time one yearling nor calf to ten cows. It is said by some of our most respectable citizens that yearlings and calves may be seen by dozens following and sucking your cows, [but the yearlings are] branded in other peoples' brand."[20]

When the letter was sent Maverick was indeed absent from San Antonio, not out of state but in west Texas surveying new property and leasing land to the federal government for new frontier forts. Since 1851 he had also been serving in the Texas legislature, where he was consumed with matters of internal improvements, education, and establishing a judicial system for the fast growing state. In June 1853 he faced six opponents for reelection but won the race and returned to Austin. In a measure of the esteem in which he was held by his peers, three years later a new county along the Rio Grande was named Maverick County.[21]

Preoccupied as Sam Maverick was, one more letter seems to have jolted his attention back to the cattle business.

It came in February 1854 from another well-known cattle dealer, William B. Grimes of Matagorda. Grimes had already tried to contact Maverick through a mutual friend, Dr. Philip Pearson. Now, "thinking from the situation of your stock on the Peninsula that you would be willing to dispose of it," he may have disconcerted Maverick with what the professional dealer thought was an appropriate offer: $2 a head, payable in thirds for up to two years. Perhaps being transparent in case Maverick had heard about it, Grimes added that he had recently purchased the remainder of Thomas DeCrow's no doubt better-maintained cattle for $4 a head on a twelve-month note, and that DeCrow had paid some of the costs of a roundup.[22]

Nearly seven years earlier Maverick had bought his cattle for $3 a head, 50 percent more than the seasoned dealer was offering. Given the price Grimes paid DeCrow, Maverick could see that if his cattle were in better control he might make a one-third profit instead of taking a one-third loss—or worse, depending on how many of his cattle could not be found.

SIX

Cattle Drive to Conquista

Less than six weeks after his lowball offer from a Matagorda cattle dealer, Sam Maverick took the option of many who find their distant holdings going sour: he decided to take personal charge of things. In March 1854, well before the full blast of the Texas summer heat, Maverick set out on horseback for Matagorda Peninsula with his two oldest sons, both on vacation from school—Sam Jr., now almost seventeen, and Lewis, nearly fifteen—plus four Mexican vaqueros. The two-month sojourn placed him in a role rarely considered by historians: trail driving.[1]

The initial plan was to move the cattle closer to home and onto a larger property by driving them from Matagorda Peninsula to Maverick's ranch on San Geronimo Creek at the edge of the Texas Hill Country, some forty miles northwest of San Antonio. They would be joining a general movement of cattle from east Texas to broader rangeland to the west.

Once back at Tiltona, Maverick and his crew had to spend a difficult three weeks rounding up strays, "a rough and hard time." They tore through brush on the peninsula all twenty-one miles south from Tiltona to DeCrow's Point and brought the herd to 250, though most of these were old, and the herd numbered far fewer than the original 400 or 450. The men hoped to find more as the drive headed north off the peninsula.[2]

On April 25 the cattle drive was at last underway, fortu-

Seven years after helping drive family cattle inland, Sam Maverick Jr. was back on horseback as an officer in the Confederate cavalry. Sam Jr. waves his canteen in this painting of the Terry Texas Rangers by Carl von Iwonski.

itously five months before a hurricane of "unparalleled fury" swept that area of the coast, leveling the town of Matagorda and sinking all ships in its harbor. Young Sam and Lewis, Maverick could report from Tiltona to their mother, "are looking well and have their appetite." Jack, now twenty-six, joined the drive along with his mother, Jinny, and a female slave named Harriet. An ox-drawn wagon hauled supplies.[3]

Maverick and his men were moving cattle at a time when long trail drives out of Texas were just beginning. Sending cattle to New Orleans on shipboard had been found generally unprofitable, and overland drives there were hindered by swamps. In 1846 a herd of Texas longhorns was driven to Missouri,

Not long after the cattle drive, Lewis Maverick, like his older brother, became a Confederate cavalry officer during the Civil War.

spurring development of a network of trails as far north as Wisconsin, Illinois, and Indiana to connect with a web of rail-heads spreading from the northeast. The technique of using a lead steer on a trail drive had been figured out, but chuck wagons were yet unknown, and other efficiencies that would allow such herds to make twelve miles a day were still being perfected. Maverick's drive, covering a much shorter distance, was lucky to make seven miles a day.[4]

"A drive calls out all a man's energy, adroitness, perseverance, and horsemanship," wrote contemporary observer Frederick Law Olmsted. Years of surveying in the wilds of west Texas had put Sam Maverick in fine shape for the ordeal, ready to share with his sons the rigors of outdoor adventure. But the cattle drive would not be altogether easy for young Sam and Lewis. By the time they reached Goliad both were recovering from illnesses, Lewis having "had chills three times."[5]

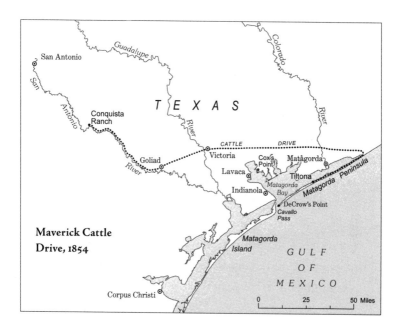

Once on the mainland the cattle turned west. They swam the short-lived canal dug around the recurring jam of logs and driftwood that blocked the Colorado River. It took some three weeks for the cattle to cross the coastal plain through Victoria and Goliad, moving 150 miles. But their destination changed, shortening the planned route by more than 80 miles. Word reached Maverick that Lipan Apaches had killed a family a few miles from the ranch on San Geronimo Creek. A safer destination, he decided, was the family's 10,500-acre Conquista Ranch forty-five miles southeast of San Antonio. It bordered a bend of the San Antonio River in newly formed Karnes County, three miles southwest of what is now Falls City. Maverick concluded that the Conquista was, after all, "the very best of places winter and summer." It straddled one end of the river's historic Conquista Ford and was also watered by the tributary Marcelina Creek.[6]

Hopes that more of Maverick's scattered cattle would turn up on the way off the peninsula proved overly optimistic, and few, if any, were found. Before reaching Goliad, Maverick added to the 250 cattle that left Tiltona by purchasing 150 more. A trail drive of 400 was comfortably within the 600 that Olmsted thought "as large a number as it is convenient to manage." Eight men and boys were riding when Maverick's cattle left the peninsula, close to the then-accepted trail ratio of four cowboys per 100 head of cattle. Whether more were added with purchase of the additional cattle is not known.[7]

From Goliad it was another fifty miles up along the San Antonio River to Conquista Ranch. That leg took another week. On May 26 father and sons were finally back in San Antonio just as a "most anxious" Mary Maverick had posted a letter begging them to return, fearing they would be caught up in the ongoing Apache raids that were driving residents from the countryside to refuge in San Antonio. Three months later Maverick and his two older sons went back to the Conquista to build a corral with fences and pens and, for Jack and his mother, a jacal, an indigenous cabin with walls of vertical sticks driven into the ground, chinked with mud and covered with a thatched roof.[8]

If Sam Maverick blamed Jack for dereliction of duty for the Tiltona herd having shrunk by more than a third instead of multiplying, he showed no sign of wanting to make a change. Jack was put in charge of the cattle once again, though it was, thought son Sam, "an absurd thing to do."[9]

The decision to keep Jack in the same role, which would ultimately spread the word *maverick* into the English language, may have had something to do with Sam Maverick's ambivalence over the institution of slavery. Maverick intensely disliked the work of supervising slaves, even of dictating choices to his own family, notes his biographer, and was as reluctant to replace Jack as he was to punish other slaves. The Mavericks could not bring themselves to practice disciplines familiar among slaveholding contemporaries. When one of their slaves was convicted of gambling and the law required him to be whipped, Maverick could not do it. In his native South Carolina, Charleston unsettled Maverick as "little better than a slave market," as he wrote his wife from there in 1845. He sensed that "there is evidently a curse hanging over a slave country, but as long as we continue in it the way is to submit to the necessity, and to use without abusing the institution."[10]

So Jack got a pass as Sam Maverick hoped for the best. But even after the cattle drive in 1854, the same troubles continued.

The ranch on San Geronimo Creek may have been the original destination because ownership of Conquista Ranch was about to be split up. The Conquista had been purchased years before with funds sent from South Carolina by Sam Maverick's father, who had died in 1852. It was to be divided in thirds among Sam Maverick, one sister, and his late other sister's heirs. Division was completed in the spring of 1856, about the time a resigned Sam Maverick at last began negotiations to sell the cattle after an offer from a neighboring rancher, Augustine Toutant-Beauregard.[11]

At Conquista Ranch, Jack justified no optimism Maverick

may have had that he could get by without help. Toutant-Beauregard reported to Maverick that Jack had told him—twice—that half the Conquista cattle were gone and only about two hundred remained. Other reports were that only a third of the cattle were branded. If correct, then less than half the cattle driven from Matagorda Peninsula would have been branded, and little if any branding would have been done at all since Maverick bought his original cattle nine years earlier.[12]

Toutant-Beauregard suggested that Jack may have been trying to discourage a sale by making the herd seem so small as to not be worth selling, either because he wanted to maintain a comfortable job "or because he does not wish you to be convinced, by counting, of the gross negligence of which he has been guilty." Toutant-Beauregard thought the true number might approach three hundred. He offered Maverick $2,000 cash for all cattle wherever they were or $7.25 per head rounded up and delivered, plus use of the jacal and corral and grazing rights on part of Maverick's third of Conquista Ranch for at least three years.[13]

Suddenly, things took another turn for the worse.

While Sam Maverick was in Austin attending the state senate session, a white hired hand appeared at the Mavericks' home in San Antonio to collect for his work at Conquista Ranch. He went back with two suits for Jack and with Sam Maverick's pistol, ostensibly to chase off three runaway slaves hiding on the ranch. Jack, meanwhile, had slipped up to San Antonio, unbeknownst to the Mavericks. When found out, he returned only after strong persuasion. Next came word from Conquista that the white hired hand was part of a gang of cattle rustlers discovered by neighboring ranchers. All were driven off. One rustler was "shot with many bullets but is alive." Jack, also accused of rustling, would be shot if he showed himself. He fled.[14]

Sam Maverick Jr. saddled his horse and rode eighty miles to his father in Austin with the news. He proposed driving the remaining cattle to San Antonio for sale to butchers, but his father preferred to deal with the offer on the table. Sam Maverick gamely countered to Toutant-Beauregard that he thought his stock at Conquista Ranch would be worth more than $3,000. But he acknowledged that Jack "is driven away, and his life threatened, &c., so that I have now no power to take any care of the stock," and so would accept $2,250 to include the horses, hogs, and wagon.[15]

Maverick sent the counteroffer letter to San Antonio for Mary Maverick's approval, which she gave. She sent the letter on to Leo Toutant-Beauregard as his father, Augustine, was away. Until Augustine returned, Maverick wrote Leo that "in the meantime it would result to the interest of your father and be greatly valued by me if you will send your herders around to gather up the stock and let it be understood you are buying them, so as to save them being run off by thieves."[16]

Maverick ended up accepting Toutant-Beauregard's original offer of $2,000—$58,000 in today's dollars—for however many cattle there happened to be. Toutant-Beauregard was to gather them wherever they could be found. No doubt to the relief of his entire family, Sam Maverick was out of the cattle business for good. Given an estimate of 450 cattle purchased at $3 a head on Matagorda Peninsula and assuming a bargain $4 a head paid for the additional 150 purchased on the drive to Conquista Ranch, the sale to Beauregard would at best have covered Maverick's total cash outlay for cattle. Revenues from the occasional sale of a few head at unspecified prices would have had little effect on the final outcome. Gone was the considerable potential profit from the perhaps hundreds of wandering calves left unbranded for others to claim.[17]

Jack eventually reappeared, free of any rustling charge, and rejoined the Maverick family. By the end of the Civil War, however, the Mavericks had sold all their adult male slaves but one. Jack went to New Orleans, lived in Kansas after emancipation, and died in San Antonio while visiting his mother, Jinny, who died in 1891 at the age of 106.[18]

The biggest single beneficiary of Sam Maverick's mavericks was the Louisiana-born Augustine Toutant-Beauregard, who had moved to Texas for his health and built up a prosperous 8,500-acre ranch bordering Conquista on the northwest. He was an older brother of Pierre Gustave Toutant-Beauregard, the Confederate general who in 1861 would order the firing on Fort Sumter. Local lore has Augustine driving a herd of his cattle, presumably including some that had been Maverick's, across the Mississippi to help feed his brother's troops.[19]

Once the deal with Sam Maverick closed, Augustine Toutant-Beauregard sent his cowboys in every direction looking for all the strays they could find. No doubt they marked many more unbranded cattle than just those that had strayed from Conquista Ranch. Who could prove otherwise?

As Toutant-Beauregard's cowboys ranged through neighboring counties on their quest, they spread the news across south Texas that any unbranded stray cattle had been Maverick's, soon making Sam Maverick an eponym—a person whose name becomes a word.

The purchaser of Sam Maverick's cattle sent cowboys like these scouring south Texas brushland to find unbranded cattle that may have been Maverick's.

The elevation took Sam Maverick into the company of Greek gods like Atlas, Roman emperors like Julius Caesar (July), and a host of such latter-day notables as James Earl Brudenell—seventh Earl of Cardigan—(sweaters), New York banker and yachtsman Elias Cornelius Benedict (guess eggs), Pittsburgh engineer George Ferris (the wheel), sixteenth-century French ambassador to Portugal Jean Nicot (nicotine), Arthur Wellesley—first Duke of Wellington—(boots), trapeze performer Jules Léotard of the tight one-piece suit, Adolph Sax of the saxophone, Julius Petri of the dish, and opera singer/foodie Louisa Tetrazzini.

Unlike the usual run of eponyms, however, the meaning of *maverick* would not be limited to its original association and would gain familiar use in dimensions far beyond unbranded cattle.

⚊ SEVEN ⚊

Tales around the Campfire

The word *maverick* was born a maverick, a yearling of an English word that leapt into the traditional Spanish range vocabulary in Texas. As its use moved with cattle up the Chisholm Trail—and others—*maverick* became embedded in the American consciousness so quickly that dim memories of its origin got almost hopelessly garbled.

Old cowhands wrote down such entertaining accounts that one can picture them as young men sitting around the campfire and gazing into flames that flickered into the mesquite smoke curling into the starlight as they competed for the tallest tale on how the word began. The yarns spun confusion persisting to this day. Did Sam Maverick brand no cattle or did he brand every stray he could find? Did he think branding was cruelty to animals? Was he trying to save money by not having to pay cowboys for branding?

Most familiar English ranching words come from Spanish. *Ranch, lariat, lasso, corral, arroyo, hacienda, burro, sombrero, stampede,* and others date from the lingo of Spanish cattlemen of the eighteenth century or before. In Spain there was a term for wild, stray, or ownerless livestock—*mostrenco, mostengo,* or *mestaña.* By the time the range lexicon migrated to Mexico and on with vaqueros into the American Southwest, the word had evolved into *mustang.* But by then its use had become limited to wild, stray, or ownerless horses. Wild, stray, or ownerless big-horn sheep in the Rocky Mountains were called *cimarrones*.[1]

When it came to describing wild, stray, or ownerless cattle, the fallback Spanish term first used by Tejanos and cowboys in California was *orejano*, "the eared one," from the term for ear, *oreja*, as one mark of cattle ownership was a cut on the ear. Other terms were *black cattle*, *Spanish cattle*, or *wild cattle*. Lexicographer Peter Watts reports that *orejano* "became the Southwestern equivalent of the Northwestern *slick-ear*, meaning an unbranded and un-earmarked cow-crittur."[2]

But *orejano* and its kin never made it into popular use in the West. It was *maverick* that Anglo and Tejano cowmen took with them up the trails into the American heartland. It came more crisply off cowboys' tongues and was unmistakably a Texas word. *Maverick*, to those who first used it, may also have been making a backhanded compliment, a good-natured jab at a well-known Texan and friend of Tejanos for breaking a fundamental rule of good ranching while still seeming to be one of the guys.

In east Texas, unbranded strays around Matagorda Bay had been recognized as Maverick's in the late 1840s. Use of the word accelerated south of San Antonio in 1856, when Augustine Toutant-Beauregard's cowboys rode into neighboring counties looking for unbranded cattle to claim as being from Sam Maverick's herd. During the Civil War, as many as 80 percent of Texas ranches were left unsupervised by men gone off to war. Branded cattle driven off by hostile Indians strayed a hundred miles or more, giving birth to calves with no one to brand them. Estimates of unbranded cattle on the Texas range ran

As few as ten trail drivers could move 2,500 cattle to railheads in Kansas.

into the millions. After the war came a scramble to reform the scattered herds and brand the unbranded.[3]

Two years later, in 1867, a massive market for Texas cattle opened up to the north. The Kansas and Pacific Railroad had reached Abilene, Kansas, where businessmen encouraged Texans to drive cattle up for shipment to the beef-hungry northeast. Texas longhorns were so hardy they could gain weight on the trail, and they required less skill and patience to handle than purebred stock.

"As trail cattle their equal has never been known and never will be," thought the celebrated cattleman Charles Goodnight. "They have at least double the endurance, and their period of life and usefulness is also about double that of any other." Trail drivers figured out how as few as ten cowboys, a cook, and a wrangler to look after saddle horses could move herds of as many as 2,500 Texas longhorns to Kansas.[4]

Cowboys scoured the state for longhorns to send up. Crews of chaps-clad "brush poppers" on horseback crashed through the south Texas undergrowth to find old unbranded steers, some of which may well have once been Sam Maverick's. Penniless cowboys could devise a brand of their own and scrounge enough mavericks to start their own herds. *Maverick* became not only a noun but a verb, for the "great era of mavericking," as one writer termed it, had begun. "It was the heyday of the open range, free grass, the long drive and, above all, the Texas Longhorn."[5]

Just as the big cattle drives began heading for Kansas, the starting gun in the Maverick Name Origin Derby was fired by the *Chicago Republican*. References to branding "mavericks" were appearing in newspapers in San Antonio in the summer of 1867, and by September the *Republican* was running its correspondent's speculation on where the term came from:

> Calves are often found a year or more old which have no brand, and as they have left their mothers cannot be identified and are taken by anyone who finds them and branded for himself. These animals are known throughout Texas as "Mavericks," the name of an extensive stock once owned by a very wealthy and influential German who, when he commenced the business of stock raising, discovered that everybody branded his cattle, and he conceived the idea that *no* brand would be a complete designation, and very economical in the way of labor; and so he adopted it, letting his cattle run without mark or brand. He learned that his stock was not to be found, while his neighbors had increased their stocks very rapidly. Hence, unbranded cattle took the name "Mavericks."[6]

San Antonio's *Daily Express* reprinted parts of the *Republican*'s larger story on Texas cattle two weeks later, noting that "in general the article is correct, but in some particulars the author has evidently gone to guess work." The *Express* editor wrote that already "we have heard many explanations of the term 'Mavericks,' but we all know it has something to do with our old friend and fellow citizen Sam Maverick, who doesn't happen to be German." The editor dodged a charge of guesswork himself by preceding details of the maverick story that were slightly askew with "we have heard" and "it is said." He concluded that Maverick "has ceased to stock raise, but his name is perpetuated in every unbranded, unmarked animal in the state." Sam Maverick, who died three years later, apparently did not respond in print to the story, leaving exaggerations to multiply.[7]

As mavericking became more and more profitable, some ranchers paid freelance cowboys by the head for whatever unbranded cattle they could turn up. Some maverickers would not brand any calf whose ownership could be in dispute. J. Frank Dobie recalled a New Mexico cowboy who "roped a bull maverick that looked to be past a year old and was about to brand it when a notoriously honest cowpuncher loped up yelling for him to wait. The puncher jumped down off his horse, grabbed the young bull's head, and went to smelling his breath. 'That yearlin' has a ma,' he said, untying the rope. 'He had his liquid diet this morning.' And, sure enough, the very next day the bull yearling, who had ranged away from his ma only temporarily, was found butting her bag for more milk."[8]

Other yearlings were not as fortunate, including many on the huge XIT Ranch, so difficult for range riders to patrol before

BRANDING A "MAVERICK," ON AN OREGON RANGE.

Mavericking became a problem throughout the Far West. This view of a maverick being branded in Oregon was published by the Portland Post Card Company about 1910.

fences. "Maverickers would ride over into the XIT pastures, find large unbranded calves, cut them off from their mothers, and run them over to their homesteads," wrote J. Evetts Haley in a history of the ranch. "Mother cows and their calves, upon becoming separated, backtrack for miles to reach the spot at which each last saw each other. The old Texas Longhorns would travel farther, guided by an uncanny sense of direction and smell [sharper] than cattle of better blood. Because of this instinct, the rustler was forced to wean the calves he stole before he applied his brand, or have them so secured that they could not return to their mothers." When no owner was in sight, the separation scene could also turn into an ugly "maverick factory," a term for "a rustler's practice of making mavericks by killing the mother with her telltale brand."[9]

With an unfenced, open range and large profits to be made from the cattle on it, mavericking became a major issue throughout the West. The ire of rightful owners against rustlers set off so many gunfights that, wrote Haley, "the trails left by the mavericks are trails blazed with human blood." Declared another: "The word 'maverick' killed more men in the Far West than any other word."[10]

Mavericking was occasionally regulated. In Palo Pinto County in Texas, cattlemen set seasonal beginning and ending dates for mavericking to equalize everyone's chances of finding mavericks and to reduce the stress on the cattle of being chased. Mavericking, wrote J. Frank Dobie, could become "a sport in which the majority of ropers prized the game more highly than the property."[11]

As the spoken-word *maverick* traveled faster than the written word, it yielded phonetic spellings like *mavrick, mavorick, mavoric,* and *mauvric.* In 1879 Colorado passed a law dealing with "Mavoricks." It set a minimum penitentiary term of one year for anyone found guilty of branding or changing the brand of cattle belonging to another and specified that district livestock associations handle disposition of "mavoricks" found in roundups. A similar law in Montana fixed the spelling. In Wyoming in 1884 a slightly different Maverick Law on how to deal with rustling led to a range conflict known as the War on Powder River that ended only when the U.S. Cavalry went in.[12]

Favorite haunts of mavericks spurred a spate of geographical place-namings across the West—of streams, peaks, gorges. Nine counties in New Mexico alone have their own Maverick Canyon. But the end of freewheeling mavericking was at hand,

The end of the "great era of mavericking" began practically in the front yard of the late Sam Maverick's home, above left in this view of Alamo Plaza, where the effectiveness of barbed wire was demonstrated in 1876. The city's open-air meat market is in the foreground, and the wooden façade around the Alamo mission's Spanish-era convento is above center. The Menger Hotel is not visible, farther off to the right.

foreshadowed in 1876 by an event in San Antonio practically in the front yard of the late Sam Maverick's home on Alamo Plaza.

Nine years earlier barbed wire had been invented in Ohio. Cattlemen did not think it would make effective fencing, and the invention had not caught on. Then promoter John W. "Bet-a-Million" Gates came to San Antonio in 1876 for a convention of cattlemen at the Menger Hotel on Alamo Plaza. He knew skeptical convention-goers were unlikely to travel out of town to see a demonstration of how barbed wire worked, even though it had recently been improved by locking simple wire barbs into a double-stranded wire. So he determined to show them right outside the hotel.

"At that time, Alamo Plaza was a mudhole," remembered Gates associate Pete McManus. "Mr. Gates and I set up the posts and strung four strands of barbed wire, making a corral of considerable size. Some of the cowboys were skeptical, and Gates and I were jollied a good deal as we went about our work of preparing for the test. A bunch of range cattle were driven into the corral and the ranchmen expected to see them go through or over the fence, but the wires held them without any trouble."[13]

After ranchers recovered from their astonishment at how barbed wire could contain cattle, orders began pouring in. By the late 1880s most of the range was no longer open. Large ranchers sealed their pastures with substantial barbed wire fences. Smaller ranchers often made do with strands strung from tree to tree, when there were trees. There are more than 2,000 variations on the 500-plus barbed wire patents. One relatively expensive type known Buckthorn involved narrow steel ribbons with jagged edges rather than separate sharp points twisted into the wire. Buckthorn was popular with sheep farmers, since wool seldom caught on it.

The transformation did produce pushbacks. In Texas, the Cowboy Strike of 1883 was caused in part by unhappiness over newly fenced ranches controlled by corporations that denied cowboys their former right to brand mavericks as part of their compensation. But the "great era of mavericking" was over.[14]

By this time the rest of the country had become captivated by romantic images of cowboys and cattle drives and shoot-outs. Cowboy slang caught on. *Maverick* was a favorite. Apparently the first nationally published story explaining the word was a twenty-eight-page article posted from San Antonio by Edward King to New York–based *Scribner's Monthly* for its January 1874 issue. King swung through town while doing articles ultimately gathered in the book *The Great South*, published before he went to the Balkans to report on the Russo-Turkish War.

One hopes that King was less a mark for the Russians and the Turks than he was for San Antonians, known for telling tall tales about their hometown. Whether King had been listening to cowboys around a campfire or jotting notes while being treated to rounds of brew at a local saloon, the result was the same. Wrote King:

The origin of the name is very funny. Col. Maverick, an old and wealthy citizen of San Antonio, once placed a small herd of cattle on an island in Matagorda Bay and, having too many other things to think of, soon forgot all about them. After a lapse of several years, some fishermen sent the colonel word that his cattle had increased alarmingly, and that there was not grass enough on the island to sustain them. So he sent men to bring them off.

There is probably nothing more sublimely awful in the whole history of cattle-raising than the story of these beasts from the time they were driven from the island until they had scattered to the four corners of West Texas. Among these Matagordian cattle which had run wild for years were 800 noble and ferocious bulls; wherever they went they found the country vacant before them. It was as if a menagerie of lions had broken loose in a village.

Mr. Maverick never succeeded in keeping any of the herd together; they all ran madly whenever a man came in sight, and

for many a day after, whenever any unbranded and unusually
wild cattle were seen about the ranges, they were called
"Mavericks."

The bulls were finally dispersed among the ranges, but they
were long the terror of the land.[15]

A quite different account appeared in what J. Frank Dobie
termed a "rollicky, reckless, realistic chronicle" by "the first authentic cowboy to publish an autobiography," in 1885. Charlie
Siringo thought of himself as "an old stove-up cowpuncher."
He was born on Matagorda Peninsula less than a year after
Sam Maverick moved his cattle away, but even being so close
to maverick's origin did not stop him from veering off into another fine campfire tale, minus the 800 raging bulls.

Said Siringo in *A Texas Cow Boy*:

As some of you may not know what a "Mavrick" is, I will try and
explain.

In [the] early days, a man by the name of Mavrick settled on
the Lavaca River and started a cow ranch. He being a chicken-
hearted old rooster, [he] wouldn't brand nor ear-mark any of his
cattle. All his neighbors branded theirs, therefore Mr. Mavrick
claimed everything that wore long ears.

When the [Civil] war broke out Mr. Mavrick had to bid adieu
to wife and babies and go far away to fight for his country's good.
When the cruel war ended, he went home and found his cattle
roaming over a thousand hills. Everywhere he went he could see
thousands upon thousands of his long-eared cattle. But when
his neighbors and all the men in the surrounding country came
home and went to branding their five years' increase, Mr. Mavrick

Kansas stockman and range historian Joseph G. McCoy thought Sam Maverick "a certain old Frenchman" who branded fifty calves for each one he actually owned.

did not feel so rich. He made a terrible fuss about it, but it did no good, as in a very few years his cattle wore some enterprising man's brand and he was left out in the cold.

Hence the term "Mavrick." At first people used to say: "Yonder goes one of Mr. Mavrick's animals!" Now they say: "Yonder goes a Mavrick!"[16]

Another perspective came from the end of the trail, where Joseph G. McCoy was a pioneer cattle-industry promoter and mayor of Abilene, Kansas; he referred to himself as the "Real McCoy," coining the term. McCoy wrote what's considered "the first book of significance pertaining to the range," *Historic Sketches of the Cattle Trade*, published in 1874. Since the correct spelling hadn't yet caught up with the spoken word in faraway Abilene, he thought it was spelled "mauvric," apparently French enough to cause McCoy to refer to Sam Maverick as "a certain old Frenchman of that name." He tripped on to imagine that this Mauvric "began raising stock with a very few head, and in a very brief space of time had a remarkably large herd of cattle. It was found that he actually branded fifty annually for each cow he owned. Of course he captured the unbranded yearlings."[17]

Then there was Anson Mills, a far west Texas pioneer and rancher credited with changing the name of the town of Franklin to El Paso. His resplendent portrait in full uniform as a brigadier general, awash in epaulets and medals, is a frontis-piece in his memoirs, which report that as a youth his principal employer in surveying was none other than Sam Maverick. Mills, however, thought Maverick as a boy had run away from home, and mixed up the cause of Maverick's imprisonment in Mexico.

It goes downhill from there. Mills next writes that Maverick "owned more cattle on the free public range than any other man in Texas. In 1861 nearly all people went into the war. Maverick's cattle ran wild on the range, and when the war closed there were tens of thousands of cattle bred during the four years. Maverick was the greatest claimant to these cattle, and marked them with his brand wherever caught. . . . It thus became the custom among cattle owners using the free range to stamp as their own any unbranded cattle they found during the 'round-up,' and to this day these stray cattle are known as 'Mavericks.'"[18]

EIGHT

Fallout from Grover Cleveland

Given the wide-ranging tales spun around the beginnings of the word *maverick*, one is left to sympathize with lexicographers and others seeking its true origins. One searcher was William Safire, Pulitzer Prize–winning *New York Times* columnist and onetime speechwriter for President Richard Nixon, who was sandbagged as he prepared *The New Language of American Politics*, published by Random House in 1968.

Six years earlier, in *Memoirs of a Maverick Publisher*, former *New York Post* publisher J. David Stern had described "old man Maverick," who "refused to brand his cattle because it was cruelty to animals." Stern wrote that Sam Maverick claimed all unbranded cattle on the range and that neighbors called him "a hypocrite, liar, and thief." Soon "lawsuits were followed by bloody battles and brought a new word to our language." Readable stuff, Safire knew as he enhanced his definition of *maverick* with Stern's words, carefully kept in quotes to leave the burden of proof on Stern. But inattentive readers paying little heed to fine points like quotation marks could believe it.[1]

Perhaps the first lexicographer to grapple with the issue was the Swedish-born Maximilian Schele de Vere, professor of modern languages at the University of Virginia for more than fifty years. "We still speak English, but we talk American," observed Schele de Vere, who lamented that obstacles to his work included "the utter indifference of the people to the minutiae of speech." His *Americanisms: The English of the New World* came out in 1872, scarcely five years after the word *maverick* began appearing in newspapers.

"A very peculiar term," wrote Schele de Vere of *maverick*, which he defined as "used in Texas to designate an unmarked yearling." He stumbled with an explanation of Sam Maverick moving to west Texas and "driving with him some three thousand head of cattle, then the largest herd in all the country," though he may have been referring to the drive west from Matagorda Peninsula to Conquista Ranch. He managed to learn that a slave had been placed in charge of branding the cattle, one "more given to the bottle than his business."

Coming so close in distant Virginia at a time when so many even in Texas had as yet little idea of these origin basics raises the question of whether Schele de Vere had buttonholed a student, William H. Maverick, Sam Maverick's fourth son, who graduated from the University of Virginia a year before Schele de Vere finished his book, or William's brother George, an earlier graduate.[2]

The broadening use of *maverick* provided a lexicographical feast. The *Dictionary of American Regional English* found *maverick* used as a verb in an early 1880s Census Office report on cattle: "The Indians stole them, the Mexicans raided them and drove them across the Rio Grande and the Texans 'mavericked' the unbranded." *Wordwizard* discovered political connotations made in 1882, when a newspaper in Fort Collins, Colorado, reported that two candidates "will soon announce themselves as political mavericks." Four years later, according to *The Oxford*

Voters in the 1904 presidential election were urged not to stray from Theodore Roosevelt, whose North Dakota ranches had used the three brands on the steer on this campaign pin.

English Dictionary, a short-lived San Francisco newspaper named nothing other than the *California Maverick* reported that one person held "'maverick views,' meaning that his views were untainted by partisanship in the matter."[3]

While in Wyoming, Owen Wister, "father of western fiction," noted "mavericking" in his journal. Theodore Roosevelt's 1888 article "Ranch Life in the Far West" told readers only that "unbranded animals are called *mavericks*," avoiding speculation on the word's origin. Sixteen years later his presidential campaign sought to keep supporters in line. The slogan "Don't Be a Maverick" rimmed a "presidential roundup" campaign pin above a red steer prominently stamped with brands Roosevelt had once registered for his ranches in North Dakota—an elkhorn, a triangle, and a Maltese cross.[4]

By 1889 *maverick* had jumped the Atlantic into John S. Farmer's *Americanisms Old and New*, published in London. Farmer gushed that "one Maverick formerly owned such immense herds that many of his animals unavoidably escaped his *rouanne* in the spring, were taken up by his neighbors, branded and called *Mavericks*. . . . No great drove can sweep through the mighty, unfenced ranch lands of the great West without drawing a wake of these *Mavericks*—these *boves per dolum amtas*—and the temptation to let them has ruined the herdsman's character."[5]

The first oil tanker built in the United States was Standard Oil Company of New York's SS *Maverick*, launched at Baltimore in 1890 with a capacity of 500,000 gallons. It had a very maverick career. For nine years it carried refined oil between Philadelphia and New England ports until it caught fire while taking on oil at Halifax, Nova Scotia. After a series of explosions the *Maverick* sank in the harbor. Once raised it took a year to maneuver it to Maine's Bath Iron Works, where the ship was rebuilt and put back into use at the end of 1900.[6]

Seven years later the *Maverick* was transferred to Standard Oil of California and took up duty along the Pacific Coast. It was sold in 1915 to a San Francisco firm formed as the Maverick Steamship Company and leased that year to a group of Germans. It became a "mystery ship" tangled in pre–World War I German plots in Southern Asia, its crew members including five "Persian waiters" who in reality were anti-British revolutionaries from India. The intended cargo was suspected to be thousands of rifles bound for anti-British German sympathizers in India. After a series of misadventures, the *Maverick* was detained by pro-British Dutch officials in the Dutch East Indies port of Batavia, now Jakarta, Indonesia. Key arrests that followed helped expose a global German conspiracy involving India. The *Maverick*, released, disappeared with its crew of twenty-five after leaving Manila for Honolulu in 1917.[7]

Discontent with the British in India had already been

The Maverick, an artists' colony at Woodstock in New York's Catskill Mountains, got this rustic theater, still in use, in 1915.

picked up by Rudyard Kipling in his 1891 story collection *Life's Handicap*. Kipling titled one chapter "The Mutiny of the Mavericks," dealing with masterless Irish soldiers seeking to foment mutiny in the ranks of the British army. As the word's use in literature spread, the next year W. S. James picked it for the subtitle of his memoir, *Cow-Boy Life in Texas, or 27 Years a Mavrick*. Dodd, Mead published works of a cowboy poet named Earl Alonzo Brininstool as *Trail Dust of a Maverick: Verses of Cowboy Life, the Cattle Range and Desert*.

Harvard-educated freethinker, writer, and socialist Hervey White established at Woodstock in New York's Catskill Mountains an artists' colony called The Maverick, its icon a wild horse—not properly a maverick but, rather, a mustang. He chose the name Maverick Press to publish his *Adventures of Young Maverick* verse collection in 1911. As the colony's cen-

A young cowboy is bucked by a snorting bull in this circa 1910 trading card of Hassan Cigarettes.

terpiece, Smith managed construction of the still acoustically sound Maverick Hall, which marked its centennial in 2015.[8]

As the glamour of the Old West caught on with the youth market, New York manufacturers of Hassan Corktip Cigarettes—"the Oriental Smoke"—featured "the Maverick" on one of their trading cards. An image of a preteen cowboy being tossed by a snorting bull was paired on the reverse with an explanation of branding, which advised that "the name Maverick comes from that of an enterprising Texan who years ago put his own brand on all the unmarked cattle he got hold of."

A reviewer of Joseph Quail's 1901 novel *Brockman's Maverick* explained that in Quail's book Maverick "is not a stray calf, but a boy," deserted by his mother. "The story chiefly concerns the heroic adventures of the Maverick in the fights which a united force of troopers and cowboys had with Indians and in other exciting occurrences on the ranch."[9]

In 1906 the pulp magazine *Brave and Bold* devoted an issue to Sam Rusher's "Young Maverick, the Boy from Nowhere." The story begins with dialogue:

By 1906 the mystique of mavericks had extended to pulp fiction.

"Where does this kid you're telling me about hail from?"

"Nowhere."

"What?"

"He says he hails from every place, and that's no place at all."

"What's his name?" . . .

"You can search me! The letters 'L. M.' are tattooed on his left forearm. . . . He calls himself Lee Maverick."

"Maverick, eh? He's the kind of a maverick that's runnin' wild with a brand. Some'un'll see him and take him in one o' these days."

Thirty-two pages later, Lee Maverick, taken in, had become "the young oil king of Texas."[10]

Such stirring fiction was preserving the mystique of a day already lost. "The changing and romantic West of the early days lives mainly in story and in song," wrote folklorist John A. Lomax in an introduction to his 1910 *Cowboy Songs and Other Frontier Ballads*. "Gone is the buffalo, the Indian warwhoop, the free grass of the open plain. . . . The trails to Kansas and to Montana have become grass-grown or lost in fields of waving grain; the maverick steer, the regal longhorn, has been supplanted by his unpoetic but more beefy and profitable Polled Angus, Durham, and Hereford cousins from across the seas." Two of the old songs Lomax collected mentioned mavericks. A third, added to a revised edition in 1938, told of Diamond Joe: "He rode the range with his cowboy band, and many a mav'rick got his brand."[11]

As cattlemen and historians sorted out the epic years of the Old West, one detail they kept having trouble with was, no surprise, the origin of the word *maverick*. "Various stories, all with very little foundation, are told as to the origin of the term," worried a history of the cattle industry in 1895. Its chapter "The Romance and Reality of the Maverick; or, Cattle Stealing as a Fine Art" went on to link Sam Maverick with the word but couldn't decide whether he was "a humane cattleman [who] declined to brand his stock on the ground that the act was brutal and unnecessary" or whether the nonbranding was due to the "drunken negligence" of a caretaker. Ten years later the landmark if strangely named history *Prose and Poetry of the Live Stock Industry*, published by the Denver and Kansas City–based National Live Stock Historical Association, added "cruel" to Maverick's supposed abhorrence of branding as brutal and unnecessary. *Prose and Poetry* provided an alternate account that got much of the story right, thanks to spreading awareness of a new telling of the story by one of Sam Maverick's sons, who lived in St. Louis.[12]

Missouri's leading Democratic newspaper at the time was the *Republic*, published in St. Louis, for decades the nation's fourth largest city and an economic magnet for the fast-developing Southwest. Its owner and editor, Charles H. Jones, had helped craft the Democratic Party's platform for the presidential election of 1888. He did not take well the defeat of his party's standard-bearer, Grover Cleveland, by the Republican, Benjamin Harrison. Resentment was especially strong in the Democratic South and in Texas, which Cleveland had carried with nearly two-thirds of the vote.

Eight days after the election, the *St. Louis Republic* ran a dispatch from its Dallas correspondent going off on Texas Republicans who had already "commenced to carve the pie" in "a scramble" for political patronage. The unidentified correspondent seemed especially annoyed at Harrison's onetime fellow Indianan and backer Edwin H. Terrell, a Texas Republican leader who "had married into a rich family" in San Antonio that "had the honor of adding a common noun to our language" thanks to the family's patriarch, a cattle thief named Sam Maverick.[13]

The correspondent explained that the Mavericks "engaged in cattle raising, and paid strict attention to business. Their herds increased with remarkable rapidity. It was their custom whenever they found a cow, steer, or calf running loose without a brand or mark to put their brand on it, and turn it among their herd." Thus "the Mavericks got rich and powerful." Moreover, the Mavericks, who originated in England, were

A political columnist called Sam Maverick a cattle thief in a critique aimed at Maverick's son-in-law Edwin Terrell, future U.S. minister to Belgium, right, one of the Texas Republicans cheered by Benjamin Harrison's victory over Grover Cleveland. The affront led Terrell's brother-in-law George M. Maverick to write what became a much-cited explanation of the origin of maverick.

reported instead to have come to Texas from Ireland; having Irish origins at the time was not particularly respectable.[14]

But one of the most stinging insults in the Old West was to call someone a cattle thief. It enraged *Republic* reader George M. Maverick, Sam Maverick's third son, who was practicing law in St. Louis and whose sister, Mary, was the wife of Edwin Terrell.

George Maverick shot back with a letter to the editor that appeared the next day. It defended Terrell's honor and declared that "he will not be a dispenser of patronage in Texas, under any circumstances—this he distinctly told me." Maverick added that "the innuendos regarding the Mavericks . . . would not be *advisedly* made by any gentleman." One can imagine affronted attorney George Maverick hand-delivering his letter, confronting abashed *Republic* editor Charles Jones, and receiving the suggestion that he respond further to the slight on the Mavericks' honor in another letter to the editor. That letter was published the next week, written, in Maverick's words, "at the solicitation of the editor, who wished to atone for an erroneous, not to say atrocious account, just previously published in his paper."[15]

Maverick's rebuttal has become a standard citation for wordsmiths. He outlined the circumstances on Matagorda Peninsula, the trail drive to Conquista Ranch, the nonbranding slave, and the sale to Toutant-Beauregard. He even devised a sort of silver lining for the family: that although ranchers may have gained ownership of Sam Maverick's cows by branding them, by calling an unbranded yearling a maverick, a cattleman "thereby erected a wide-spreading monument of gratitude to his benefactor."[16]

But he seems to have fallen short in his declaration that "of the thousand and one versions of the story only one can be correct. Be assured this is the true account." In his letter George Maverick asserted that Sam Maverick took the cattle only to settle a debt, "as it was a case of cattle or nothing." This is the first such statement that can be found, and it has been repeated ever since. Yet no contemporary documents mention a debt or suggest that the transaction was anything other than a cash transaction, as testified by George Maverick's oldest brother, Sam Jr., and by their mother in her memoirs. Nor do the numbers of cattle and dollar amounts George Maverick presents agree with documented totals. But the rest of his account mostly squares with the historical record.[17]

And so it was, improbably, that fallout from the defeat of Grover Cleveland precipitated our earliest authoritative discourse published on the word *maverick*, an account that could inoculate future generations against wildly erroneous stories—if future generations were paying attention.

Hoping to preserve his letter's impact, George Maverick reprinted it in 1905 as a pamphlet, which itself was reprinted three decades later by his daughter Rena Maverick Green. But those reading it could still slip up. The celebrated Texas folklorist J. Frank Dobie quoted from the pamphlet in his 1936 classic *The Longhorns*, still in print. But when Dobie read "DeCrow's Point on Matagorda Bay" he apparently did not realize DeCrow's Point was on Matagorda Peninsula, as an even more accessible source—Mary Maverick's *Memoirs*, first published fifteen years earlier—had specified. Dobie instead put Maverick's cattle across from Matagorda Peninsula onto Matagorda Island and proceeded to poetically describe the incorrect setting.[18]

Ten years later Green Peyton's *San Antonio: City in the Sun* moved Maverick's cattle even farther south, to St. Joseph's Island. Dobie got Maverick's unbranded cattle onto the Texas mainland by having them walk across at low tide. Peyton came up with a sandbar that "presently washed up between the island and the mainland." In fact, since the cattle were never on Matagorda Island or St. Joseph's Island but on Matagorda Peninsula, the long spit of land north of both islands, all the cattle had to do was wander to the mainland on dry ground.[19]

C. L. Douglas's entertaining *Cattle Kings of Texas*, like *The Longhorns* also still on bookstore shelves, "represents two years of painstaking effort, countless interviews and the ceaseless poring over of old documents, records and scrap books," the editor of *The Cattleman* magazine, first publisher of the stories, assured readers in 1935. "Each chapter has been checked and rechecked by various individuals, often relatives and associ-

San Antonio congressman James L. Slayden, shown at left during planting of a tree on the Capitol grounds, spoke on the floor of Congress in 1919 about the "ridiculous lies" regarding the origin of maverick.

ates of the subject." Yet Douglas's chapter "The Mavericks of Matagorda" illustrates the wrong Maverick brand and misses and misstates basic facts reported correctly in sources he cites.[20]

Nor, again, could the family be depended on to get everything right. James L. Slayden, married to a sister of Sam Maverick's son Albert's wife, represented San Antonio in Washington for twenty-two years. In a windy valedictory address that spread across nearly a full page of the *San Antonio Evening News* in 1919, Congressman Slayden accompanied a review of his career with a lengthy discourse on his state's history and legends. It included the observation that "another and even more interest-ing case of perverted history is that of Samuel A. Maverick."

Slayden went into George Maverick's revision of common tales and would have been pretty much okay had he not some-how identified Sam Maverick as "a civil engineer by profession," apparently confusing Maverick's work as a surveyor with engi-neering. The portion of Slayden's speech about the word *maverick* was picked up by newspapers as far away as Boston and may have planted the seed for the definition of Sam Maverick as "a Texas engineer and rancher" that would spring up on the *Oxford Dictionary's* website, thwarting Slayden's declaration: "This, Mr. Chairman, is the true story of the origin of the word 'maverick' as applied to unbranded cattle, and I hope that its publication in the [*Congressional*] *Record* will end forever the ridiculous lies."[21]

The weight of the *Congressional Record* was, alas, insufficient to stifle the "thousand and one versions of the story" George Maverick had tilted at three decades earlier. It fell on a lat-ter-day former San Antonio congressman, George Maverick's nephew Maury, to go on the attack when Sam Maverick was called a cattle thief.

In 1952 several members of the Maverick family had tried to get the Albuquerque printing firm of Babcock & Borough to change the wording of a printed slip enclosed with boxes of its Maverick Stationery, featuring a series of drawings by cowboy artist George Phippen. The slip, "The Story of the Maverick," elaborated on one version of an erroneous tale and asserted that "Mr. Maverick had an aggravating habit of rounding up and claiming unbranded calves anywhere he found them, and herding them over the famous Chisholm Trail to the Kansas beef markets." The complainants got no response. Maury Maverick, in retirement, heard about it and took on the case. He rarely went halfway on anything.

"The story which you so widely disseminate is wholly fabricated and false," Maverick thundered in a letter to Babcock & Borough. "There is absolutely not a word of truth in your story and no honest or sensible person who has made research can believe a word of it. . . . You have no more business referring to my grandfather as a thief than I have referring to the Babocks and Boroughs as the grandchildren of thieves." Maverick went on to explain the origin of the word ("Why not tell the true story?"), praised the drawings by the artist, and asked the company to redo its slip and "no longer send out the libel and slander that insults my family."

Maverick sent a letter to the artist, complimenting the art but asking him, too, to do something about the situation and wondering if he thought it would be fair if a story suggesting the artist's grandfather was a thief was widely distributed throughout the nation.

A third letter went to Maverick's friend Stanley Marcus, head of Neiman Marcus, the high-end Dallas department store that carried the stationery. Stanley Marcus promptly replied that he was "shocked by the discovery of the offending paragraph." He wrote Maverick that he had the slips removed from all unsold boxes and had advised the printer that Neiman Marcus would purchase no more stationery unless that slip was no longer included.

That did it. The printer suddenly responded to everyone,

blaming the cowboy writer S. Omar Barker for getting it wrong in the first place and hoping that his correction would suffice. Barker's new effort described the transfer of Maverick's cattle to Augustine Toutant-Beauregard: "ol' Toot told his cowpokes to slap his brand on every unbranded bovine they bumped into."

That was too much for Maury Maverick. "Toutant de Beauregard was never at any time referred to as 'ol' Toot,'" Maverick fired back, perhaps annoyed by a real or imagined implication of flatulence, and he lectured the printer about unauthentic vernacular as well. Maverick pointed out that Beauregard's grandson was serving as an admiral in the U.S. Navy and scolded that "the story which you now write instead of making a thief out of my grandfather makes a thief out of the admiral's grandfather."[22]

NINE

The Maverick Gene

There were Mavericks who were mavericks before the word and Mavericks who were mavericks after the word gained currency. In twentieth-century San Antonio, two unconventional Mavericks—Maury Sr. and Maury Jr.—made local and national political headlines for more than seven decades. Newspaper columnist Rick Casey checked back to the 1600s and found the Samuel Maverick who fell out with the Puritans in Massachusetts. Casey made the connections and came up with a dynastic "Maverick prototype: a member of the establishment who marches to a different drummer."[1]

The Maverick family does not make lists of American dynasties that are most prominent or powerful or socially elite. Indeed, trying to gather Mavericks into a single category would be akin to herding cats. But a case can be made for ranking the Mavericks more broadly as a distinctive American family that has maintained an identity for thoughtfully going its own way since the initial English settlement. Samuel Maverick of the Massachusetts Bay Colony was the first to fit the definition of the word even before it was invented.

"Many such 'mavericks' settled America before 1630," said one historian of colonial America, adding that "altogether these earliest English settlers added color and variety to the cultural mosaic of early America." Such traits did not often make it down through many generations as they have in the Maverick family. Through the years some Mavericks have been more maverick than others, raising the paradox of maverick Mavericks. But if one were looking for a progenitor to set the tone of such a family for the next four centuries, one would have to look no further than the first American Samuel Maverick.[2]

"Most of the Fathers of Massachusetts wore a grim and forbidding aspect," wrote Devonshire historian Beatrix Cresswell. "Samuel Maverick in strong contrast was full of geniality and friendship towards all he met." He was born in 1602 in southwestern England. His father, the Rev. John Maverick, sympathized with Puritan Separatists and later immigrated with a group of them to Massachusetts. He became the second minister of what is now First Parish Church in Dorchester, then Congregationalist and later Unitarian.[3]

Samuel Maverick was thirteen when his father, an Anglican curate, was named rector of a tiny church in Beaworthy, in a corner of Devonshire so remote that Cresswell thought that "as a residence for a man of scholarly tastes, such as John Maverick seems to have possessed, it must have been exile indeed." Beaworthy's "one local event was an annual fair on July 25th, of which the principal feature was a race of old women for a greased pig." Added Cresswell: "All that can be said is that a minister who resided there fourteen years would have been able to adapt himself far more easily to life in the recently founded settlements of New England than many of his clerical brethren."[4]

Samuel Maverick came to Massachusetts in 1624, six years

BOSTON FUSILEERS, IN FRONT OF THE MAVERICK HOUSE, EAST BOSTON.

East Boston's Maverick House, a hostelry once owned by the grandfather of John F. Kennedy, long dominated Maverick Square, south of Samuel Maverick's 1636 home site.

before his parents, and settled at the mouth of the Mystic River at Winnissimett, now Chelsea, to live within a small land grant intended for Anglicans. He began trading with Indians along the coast and tending to lands he purchased elsewhere in Massachusetts, including in what is now Maine. Rather than joining his father and the Puritan majority in setting up a sort of theocracy, Samuel Maverick held to the established Church of England. Consequently, the editor of Governor John Winthrop's journal points out, Maverick was "on account of his Episcopal leanings looked upon askance in the community, where, though recognized as a man of substance and worth, he was given no public place."[5]

Maverick kept away from the crowd by moving with his wife, Amias, and their family to 663-acre Noddle's Island, named for early settler William Noddle and one of several harbor islands that made up East Boston. Noddle's Island became more accessible when connected to the mainland by landfill in the early twentieth century. In 1636 Samuel Maverick bought the island and built a house, fortified with four small cannons. The site of his home is just north of present-day Maverick Square, reached via the Massachusetts Bay Transportation Authority's Blue Line subway at Maverick Station, one stop from Logan Airport.[6]

On Noddle's Island, Maverick could avoid the dourness of so many of his fellow citizens and enjoy being, in the words of one contemporary, "of a very loving and courteous behavior, very ready to entertain strangers," yet, in religion, "an enemy to the reformation at hand." One traveler found him "the only hospitable man in all the country, giving entertainment to all comers gratis." Despite religious differences, Maverick's guests included the Puritan governor, John Winthrop.[7]

In 1638 Samuel Maverick became "one of the earliest (if not *the* earliest) slaveholders in Massachusetts," wrote mid-nineteenth-century East Boston historian William H. Sumner. He bought two slaves from a ship captain up from the Caribbean even though slavery was still "repugnant to the feelings of Puritans, and was looked upon with abhorrence." Forty years later there were more than one hundred slaves in Massachusetts, a small fraction of those in colonies to the south. Sumner added that "the whole subject was looked upon in an entirely different light from what it now is."[8]

Friendly though Maverick remained with many Puritan leaders and trusted though he may have been in civic matters short of holding office, as a royalist he "seems generally to have been at war with the government," wrote Sumner. His reports on disloyal actions of Puritan colonists contributed to the London government's view that New England was more trouble than it was worth. In Massachusetts, Maverick kept insisting there be equal rights for those other than Puritans. In turn, he faced increasing accusations from Puritans of legal infractions. One charge was for harboring one man and the wife of another who had escaped imprisonment on charges of illicit conduct. Three men were fined "for abuseing themselves disorderly with drinkeing to much strong drink" aboard the *Friendship* and at Maverick's house, though some maintained that the drinking occurred only on the ship. Fears that Maverick plotted with guests to replace the Puritan government with royalist rule caused him to be ordered to leave Noddle's Island and move to Boston, an order shortly withdrawn.[9]

Maverick and four others were jailed in 1647 for preparing and gathering signatures for a petition to be sent to London complaining of their being denied full civil and religious rights—even the ability to baptize their children—in violation of the laws of England. When discovered, the Boston court found the petitioners guilty of conspiracy and perjury. Maverick refused to pay his substantial fine and tried transferring title to Noddle's Island to his son in case it might be seized as payment. Although the fine was later halved, Maverick was sufficiently discouraged by the experience to sell the island anyway, in 1650, and move onto the mainland.[10]

By this time the monarchy had been overthrown, Charles I was executed, and the Puritan-favored Calvinist Oliver Cromwell was in charge. Any chance of anti-Puritan redress in Massachusetts was now unlikely. But once the monarchy was restored to Charles II in 1660 and the Church of England was reestablished, Samuel Maverick thought it time for him to go to England and express directly to the king his displeasure with his treatment by the locals. He took with him his pioneering *A Briefe Discription of New England and the Severall Townes Therein, Together with the Present Government Thereof,* which he may have presented to the king's lord high chancellor. The manuscript is the first known account of New England written by a longtime resident rather than by a traveler passing through. Its unique historical details created a sensation when found at the British Museum in 1884.[11]

Samuel Maverick returned to Boston in 1664 with an appointment by Charles II as one of four royal commissioners charged with sorting out complaints in the colonies and, in particular, with seeing that New Amsterdam was taken from the Dutch, with whom the English were frequently at war. Maverick wasted little time in brandishing authority over his former tormentors—the Puritan government of Massachusetts finally lost its charter twenty years later—but he soon moved to New York, the former New Amsterdam. There his work so pleased the Duke of York, who would become James II, that Maverick was given a home at 50 Broadway, now the site of a thirty-seven-story office building, where it is thought Maverick died about 1670.[12]

There had been no fewer than three Samuel Mavericks living in Massachusetts at the same time—Samuel Maverick of Noddle's Island, his son Samuel Maverick, and a nephew named Samuel Maverick. A century later yet another Samuel Maverick surfaced, one who also got at cross-purposes with authority, this time as the American Revolution was brewing.[13]

This Samuel Maverick was seventeen and apprenticed to an ivory turner in Boston as friction grew between the British and colonials disenchanted with British rule. By 1770 he was associating with colonial radicals. On the night of March 5 he was having supper with friends when a bell rang out. Thinking there was a fire, the youths went to investigate. They joined a crowd heading toward the Custom House, where, instead of a blaze, eight armed British soldiers in red uniforms were being taunted. One frightened soldier fired, hitting no one but throwing the mob into tumult. Maverick, among others, ran toward the line of soldiers. According to one account he cried, "Fire away, you damned lobsterbacks!" They did, quickly. A ricocheting musket ball hit Samuel Maverick. He was taken to his widowed mother's boarding house, where he died a few hours later.[14]

Four others also died, and six were wounded in what colonial newspapers promptly termed a "massacre." Most shops in Boston and neighboring towns were shut and all bells "ordered to toll a solemn peal" as more than ten thousand mourners followed horse-drawn hearses to the Granary Burying Ground, where a grave marker remains. In the row of block prints portraying coffins in the *Boston Gazette*, Samuel Maverick's

An engraving of the 1770 Boston Massacre by Paul Revere memorializes the shooting of Samuel Maverick and the other victims.

displays a scythe and an hourglass, signifying a life cut short before its time. A colored engraving made three weeks after the Boston Massacre by Paul Revere skews the scene to exaggerate brutality by the British soldiers and has been termed "probably the most effective piece of war propaganda in American history."[15]

Last Thursday, agreeable to a general Request of the Inhabitants, and by the Consent of Parents and Friends, were carried to their *Graves* in Succession, the Bodies of *Samuel Gray, Samuel Maverick, James Caldwell*, and *Crispus Attucks*, the unhappy Victims who fell in the bloody Massacre of the Monday Evening preceeding!

On this Occasion most of the Shops in Town were shut, all the Bells were ordered to toll a solemn Peal, as were also those in the neighboring Towns of Charlestown Roxbury, &c. The Procession began to move between the Hours of 4 and 5 in the Afternoon; two of the un-

The Boston Gazette *portrayed Samuel Maverick's coffin with a scythe and hourglass to signify a life cut short before its time.*

Soon the Maverick surname was fading from view in the Northeast, with the notable exception of a New York family of engravers and silversmiths established in the late eighteenth century by Peter Rushton Maverick, whose forebears immigrated after their Boston Maverick cousins. Patriarch Samuel Maverick's son Nathaniel left Boston for the Caribbean commercial hub of Barbados, and Nathaniel's son went on to Charleston, where, four generations of Samuels later, the latest Samuel Maverick and his son Samuel Augustus joined earlier Mavericks in presaging the meaning of *maverick*, this time by openly opposing the doctrine of states' rights in the secessionist hotbed of South Carolina.[16]

What seems to be a Maverick gene for being unbranded kept passing down through the generations with predictable

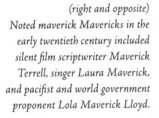

(right and opposite)
Noted maverick Mavericks in the
early twentieth century included
silent film scriptwriter Maverick
Terrell, singer Laura Maverick,
and pacifist and world government
proponent Lola Maverick Lloyd.

unpredictability, contrasting some Mavericks with others who
were less so. Lola Maverick Lloyd got the gene and became
a nationally known social activist in world peace, world government, and women's movements in the era before and after
World War I. Her uncle Sam Maverick Jr., on the other hand,
was a Confederate cavalry hero in Terry's Texas Rangers. Lola
Lloyd became matriarch of a family of pacifists and social activ-
ists, among them Georgia Lloyd, longtime executive secretary
of the Campaign for World Government. Florence Maverick
Kelley, an advocate for legal rights for the poor, in 1960 was
the first woman named chief judge of what became the Family
Court in New York City, her work contrasting with that of corporate lawyer cousins like Albert Maverick III, deputy general
counsel for Houston's Brown & Root.

Maverick Terrell cut a path as a screenwriter in 1916 by collaborating on scripts with Charlie Chaplin. His first cousin Laura Maverick sang in the maverick niche of mezzo-contralto, between mezzo-soprano and contralto, a term now little used. Alden Erikson was a prolific *Playboy* cartoonist in the 1960s and 1970s, while his third cousin William Maverick Griswold rose through institutional ranks to direct New York's Morgan Library and Museum and, in 2014, was named director of the Cleveland Museum of Art.

Few comparisons within the Maverick family, though, are as stark as those between one of Sam Maverick's grandsons and one of his nephews, son of his sister Lydia Maverick Van Wyck. "To hell with reform!" was a campaign theme of Robert A. Van Wyck, picked by Tammany Hall as the Democratic candidate

in 1897 for mayor of New York, the first since consolidation of its five boroughs. After Van Wyck won, his administration was scarred by corruption, though he oversaw the beginning of New York's subway system and is remembered in the naming of the Van Wyck Expressway in Queens. In 1898 the Democratic nominee for governor of New York was Robert's brother Augustus, narrowly defeated by Theodore Roosevelt.[17]

At the opposite end of the mainline political spectrum were the Van Wycks' first cousin once removed, Maury Maverick, passionately devoted to reform, and his son, Maury Jr., a liberal Texas legislator and candidate for the U.S. Senate in 1961. Maury Sr. once said he opposed birth control on the grounds that it would have caused him not to have been born, as he was the youngest of eleven children of Sam Maverick's son Albert and Virginia-born Jane Maury Maverick. Twice elected as a New Deal congressman and once as mayor of San Antonio, he was a favorite of the nation's liberals and stirred things up wherever he went.

Maverick cousins at opposite ends of the political spectrum were conservative New York mayor Robert Van Wyck (opposite left) and his brother, New York gubernatorial candidate Augustus Van Wyck (opposite right); and liberal congressman Maury Maverick (left), who backed the United Auto Workers in Detroit, and his son, Maury Maverick Jr., who used a Texas longhorn campaign pin (above) during his 1961 run for the U.S. Senate.

TEN

Maury Maverick
and Gobbledygook

If anyone personified the definition of the word *maverick* in the twentieth century, it was Maury Maverick. He's described as everything from "a human whirlwind" to "a Texas norther in Congress." His career so closely paralleled that of New York's dynamic mayor Fiorello La Guardia that in 1939 the *New York Daily News* thought "Maverick talks like La Guardia and thinks like him" and wondered "whether this is a Texas La Guardia or La Guardia is a New York Maverick."

Maverick biographer Richard B. Henderson observed that both "were short and squat; both were of the 'stormy petrel' type; both had been heroes in World War I, La Guardia in the air and Maverick on the ground; both had led liberal blocs in the U.S. House of Representatives; and both had been defeated for Congress only to emerge as cleanup mayors of their home cities."[1]

Once he took his seat in Congress in 1935, Maury Maverick had "unquestionably, the most meteoric rise in Congress during the New Deal," believed one observer. Another, J. August Wolf, writing in the *St. Louis Post-Dispatch Magazine*, said Maverick took "a running broad jump onto the nation's front pages," then described him in action: "His five feet and a little over

Congressman Maury Maverick, a strong ally of Franklin D. Roosevelt, pointed out scenes in front of the Alamo to the president during a visit to San Antonio in 1936.

are not impressive. But his resounding voice rolls out from his barrel chest and his words ring up into the House galleries. His round face grows red with conviction as he unloosens a stinging accusation, and then his blue eyes pop with mischief as he swings to raillery."[2]

Maverick's biographer counted him as the primary subject of sixteen items in the *New York Times* during his first year compared with nine about the majority leader. He organized liberal Democratic friends into a bloc known as the Mavericks, more enthusiastic for the New Deal than the House's conservative Democratic leadership, and "his unmatched candor and audacity, even when dealing with the president, became the talk of Washington." As a rare liberal congressman from the

South, Maury Maverick championed organized labor and supported a minimum-wage law, the Tennessee Valley Authority, and Franklin D. Roosevelt's plan to expand the Supreme Court to achieve favorable rulings. British journalist Alistair Cooke thought him "nothing but a maverick." Harry Truman thought "Maury's ideas were like ripples on a pond—everyone around was influenced to some degree by him."[3]

In 1938 Maverick was defeated in the Democratic primary for a third term in the House, losing by less than 500 of the 50,000 votes cast. The *Baltimore Sun* saw Maverick's problem as having been more "Roosevelt than Roosevelt." Opposition to the New Deal was growing in Texas and elsewhere, and several other members of the Maverick bloc lost reelection as well. He promptly ran for mayor of San Antonio, won, and was sworn in by his father, Albert, on May 13, 1940, one hundred years from the date his grandfather, Sam Maverick, began his first term as mayor.[4]

Maury Maverick had no fear of treading on toes as he oversaw numerous municipal administrative reforms, upgraded health standards, got funding to begin San Antonio's international airport, and achieved completion of a major historic preservation project—La Villita—and the San Antonio River Walk. But he narrowly lost reelection in 1941. The loss was due in part to negative reaction over Maverick's having given the Communist Party permission to meet in San Antonio's Municipal Auditorium, done in his firm belief that "the right of assembly and the expression of unpopular belief are the bases for the preservation of democracy." Not granting the request, he said, would have been "going against everything I've stood for all my life."[5]

Despite volleys of police tear gas and streams of water, an angry mob of 5,000—some bused in—broke up the rally. Police helped the cluster of Communists escape out a rear door. Mob members, furious at having missed them, vandalized the auditorium, slashed fire hoses, and hanged Maverick in effigy. Meanwhile the local Ku Klux Klan was looking for Maverick at the family compound on Sunshine Ranch seven miles away, though Maverick and his wife, Terrell, were not there. Nearly eighty years later Maverick's niece Ellen Maverick Clements Dickson, then nine, could vividly remember that night.[6]

"Our parents were away, so my younger sister Jamie and I were spending the night with our grandparents up the hill," Ellen Dickson recalled. "We heard the Klan coming. I'll never forget those men in their white hoods and robes as they stood outside, shining their flashlights through the windows and around the rooms looking for Uncle Maury. When they left, my grandparents sent us to stay with cousins in a small rock house down the hill. My grandparents lived in a large frame house, and I guess they were afraid the Klan might come back and burn it down."[7]

"The riot was probably the worst exhibition of Nazi activities that has ever taken place in the United States," Maverick later told the *San Antonio Express*. "I do not think the reaction has been good politically; however, I have no regrets. If I had it to do again, I would do it again." He received a torrent of editorial support, from Virginius Dabney in the *Richmond Times-Dispatch* to the usually conservative *Dallas Morning News*.[8]

Maverick's temper over the fray did not soon cool. His son, Maury Jr., then eighteen, recounted a time not long after when he accompanied his father to St. Mark's Episcopal Church.

After the service ended, Maverick was shaking hands with the rector when "one of San Antonio's most important 'high society' women came up and in a loud voice accosted him with the comment, 'Why, Maury Maverick, what are you doing in church? I've heard talk around town that you are a communist, but I guess you couldn't be if you go to the Episcopal Church.'

"Poor old papa's face went livid. With the voice that would have been the envy of a drill sergeant he said back to the woman, 'I hear talk around town that you are an old whore, but I guess you couldn't be if you go to the Episcopal Church.' Episcopalians began to scatter like chickens, the preacher rolled his eyes in back of his head and I damn near wet my pants."[9]

With war at hand, Maverick found himself back in Washington going through management positions in price administration and war production. He maintained his strenuous schedule of speaking engagements throughout the country. Many talks were on themes outlined in his 1937 autobiographical best-seller, *A Maverick American*, which *Time* magazine termed a "rambling, engaging, man-to-man discourse" by a "literate legislator." The book was laced with a healthy dose of references to Maverick forebears, most of whom, fortunately, had been on the right side of history. These included the Puritan-era Samuel Maverick, who, Maury Maverick reminded a Boston audience, had been "in continuous hot water with your authorities because he believed in civil and religious liberties." In New York, he caught Mayor La Guardia with the question of who named the city of New York and exulted that it was the same Samuel Maverick, while he was one of England's royal commissioners charged with taking New Amsterdam from the Dutch in 1664.[10]

Also mentioned in *A Maverick American* was a family tie to another eponymous word. Charles Lynch, a Virginia planter, patriot, and judge, was a great-great-uncle of Sam Maverick's wife, Mary, and brother of the founder of Lynchburg. Charles Lynch meted out harsh and precipitous sentences to Loyalists in Revolutionary times, yielding the word *lynch*.[11]

Although the bullish, brash, and irreverent image Maury Maverick projected was good for getting votes, it obscured what biographer Richard Henderson detected as "a great respect for scholarship and the scholars." As a teenager Maverick studied the books he read—primarily political and social histories—and was coached by his father in the lessons of free inquiry and freedom of expression. He left San Antonio without completing high school to spend a year at Virginia Military Institute, then returned to the state for two years in a prelaw curriculum at the University of Texas.[12]

Maverick "not only found his courses to be dull and turned to his own reading list, but also spent considerable time in frivolity and roistering about the campus" and received poor grades. He nevertheless spent his later life building a wide-ranging library and filling margins of its books with extensive notes. An insatiable curiosity fueled "his capacity for original thought." This veered into word invention in 1937 when a prize was offered at a Chicago hotel show for a word easier on the American tongue than *hors-d'oeuvres*. One entry was "horse-doovers." The prize went to a New Orleans man for "apiteaser."[13]

The subject stirred up a national exchange. Maverick got into the fun by coming up with "dingle-doo." One newspaper, Michigan's *Battle Creek Enquirer*, told readers that Maverick "explained he was interested only in fixing things so a hungry man at a party can get something to eat without needing a French accent." The well-known New York and Chicago restaurateur George Rector came back by telling the *Washington Star* that hors d'oeuvres should instead be named "mavericks," since "a maverick is something that does not belong anywhere in particular and any man can put his brand on it if he can catch it. And that fits the old-time free lunch as well as the fancy appetizers in the fanciest hotel in the country."[14]

Neither that twist on *maverick* nor *apiteaser* nor any of the other alternatives, however, successfully made it into the language. *Dingle-doo* was chronicled in supplemental volumes of Maverick's friend H. L. Mencken's monumental *The American Language* but otherwise appeared only in a few scholarly journals and arcane publications. It would be another few years before one of Maverick's linguistic inventions burst into common use.[15]

Maverick's job in war production management was earning him respect as "an able, vigorous administrator." When he was named chairman in January 1944 of the Smaller War Plants Corporation, charged with bringing more small businesses into defense production, Adlai E. Stevenson, then special assistant to the secretary of the navy, wrote Maverick that his appointment was "the first good home front news I have heard in a long while."[16]

Maverick was pleased with his new office, which, he wrote a friend, "is really the most beautiful of any government office in the United States of America." There were "about four windows which face on the Capitol, directly in front of me, as an unobstructed view. . . . It's a fine thing to sit here and look up

SMALLER WAR PLANTS CORPORATION
Washington, D.C.

TO: Everybody in Smaller War Plants Corporation   March 24, 1944

FROM: Maury Maverick, Chairman & Gen. Manager

SUBJECT: Lengthy Memoranda and Gobbledygook Language.
         Be short and use Plain English.

Memoranda should be as short as clearness will allow. The
Naval officer who wired "Sighted Sub - Sank Same" told the
whole story.

Put the real subject matter - the point - and even the conclusion, in the opening paragraph and the whole story on
one page. Period! If a lengthy explanation, statistical
matter, or such is necessary, use attachments.

Stay off gobbledygook language. It only fouls people up.
For the Lord's sake, be short and say what you're talking
about. Let's stop "pointing-up" programs, "finalizing"
contracts that "stem from" district, regional or Washington
"levels". There are no "levels" - local government is as
high as Washington Government. No more patterns, effec-
tuating, dynamics. Anyone using the words "activation"
or "implementation" will be shot.

Maury Maverick's 1944 memo that gave birth to the word gobbledygook *is in the National Archives.*

at the Capitol. I can see the flags flying in the breeze. Out on the street there are soldiers and sailors and Marines walking back and forth from the station. The sun seems to glitter on the trees. I see an airplane flying almost, it seems, right in front of my window."[17]

But as Maury Maverick got down to business, it took scarcely two months for his exasperation with obfuscation in writing and expression to boil over.

"Lengthy Memoranda and Gobbledygook Language" was the subject line of the memo dated March 24, 1944, that Maverick sent his entire staff, followed by the directive "Be short and use Plain English." Its three terse paragraphs pleaded, "For the Lord's sake, be short and say what you're talking about."

He instructed that "memoranda should be as short as clearness will allow. The Naval officer who wired 'Sighted Sub—Sank Same' told the whole story. . . . Put the real subject matter—the *point*—and even the conclusion, in the opening paragraph and the whole story on one page. Period! If a lengthy explanation, statistical matter, or such is necessary, use attachments. Stay off gobbledygook language. It only fouls people up."[18]

Response to the memo was electric. The day after it went out it was reprinted and praised by a *Washington Post* columnist as "the most refreshing—and effective, I predict—memo ever written in the federal service." Newspapers throughout the country picked up the story. The *Cleveland Plain Dealer* joked, "O.K., Maury, we'll implement your suggestion as soon as it has been activated and channelized by the proper authorities." Jack Stinnett's syndicated "Washington in Wartime" column reported, in the *Duluth News Tribune* and other papers, that "no sooner had Maverick's memo made the rounds than Rear Adm. W. B. Young, chief of the navy bureau of supplies and accounts, had it reprinted and circulated to his staff with the brief paraphrase: 'Sighted memo—agree to same.'"[19]

In California, the *Oakland Tribune* reported that the gobbledygook memo inspired the Federal Security Agency to circulate one of its own, urging its staff to get in line: "A horrible example quoted is this: 'The forms are obsolete and should be consigned to the receptacles used in disposing of your daily accumulations of trash.' Seemingly, it had occurred to no one to say, 'The forms are out of date, throw them away.'"[20]

"I've never seen such a response to anything in my life," Maverick wrote a month later to Lester Markel, then Sunday

A Washington bureaucrat deluged with newly defined gobbledygook *got a sympathetic portrayal in the* New York Times.

editor of the *New York Times*. Markel was preparing to run Maverick's article "The Case against 'Gobbledygook'" in the *Times Sunday Magazine* on May 21. "Our clipping service, which is totally inadequate, has accumulated two or three hundred editorials," wrote Maverick. "The War Department told me that they were using it in the European overseas issues of 'Stars and Stripes.'" The *Times* article gave Maverick an opportunity to explain how the word came to him and why it caught on.[21]

> Recently, when I became chairman of the Smaller War
> Plants Corporation, torrents, yea, verily, tidal waves of
> papers, documents, memoranda, clippings and letters swirled
> around me. I was drowning. Thus came my second revolt. In
> righteous indignation I rattled off a memorandum denouncing
> gobbledygook language. People asked me how I got the word. I

do not know. Perhaps I was thinking of the old bearded turkey gobbler back in Texas who was always gobbledygobbling and strutting with ridiculous pomposity. At the end of his gobble there was a sort of gook.

The response to the memorandum was immediate and widespread. Letters poured in showing that the American people are tired of double-talk and talk they can't understand. No one regarded the tyranny of words as funny. I was even asked to write this story about it, and I do so in deadly earnestness. . . . Memos should be short and to the point. If the executive has to struggle through tiresome, wordy memoranda on his desk, they pile as high as the sky, creating a Great Slow Down Wall. Sometimes the job is never done, memos being written until the problem blows up in your face. Then it is too little and too late. . . .

I have a hunch that a writer, feeling defeat in advance, gets lengthy and vague in self-defense. If defeat comes, he can hide behind the big words and ascribe it to the ignorance of the people addressed. . . . Anyone who is thinking clearly and honestly can express his thoughts in words which are understandable, and in very few of them.[22]

In this piece and later, Maverick hedged on exactly how he was inspired to come up with that specific word. Lexicographers smelled a rat. "Maverick may have been disingenuous, or the *Times* may have been adhering to its policy of only publishing news that is fit to print," sensed a writer in the *Chronicle of Higher Education*, Ben Yagoda. "But in any case, Maverick's etymology was, at best, incomplete, as *gobbledygoo* [no 'k'] had a long-established meaning at the time," denoting a prostitute's practice of fellatio. Added Yagoda: "Try to keep *that* out of your mind the next time a colleague goes on about 'optimization of best practices going forward.'" The possibility of Maverick's familiarity with *gobbledygoo* squares with Maverick's biographer's report that "his private speech was extremely earthy." John Ayto's *Twentieth Century Words* may have gotten it right: "Presumably it was the sound of the word (suggestive of a fatuous turkey) that drew Maverick to it, rather than its meaning."[23]

Whatever the origin of the root, by adding the "k" Maverick had in fact come up with a new word. The gobbling of turkeys resonated as a metaphor with those frustrated with the verbosity of so many bureaucrats. The *Times* article and its republication in *Reader's Digest* stepped up the volume of reaction that first followed the memo. William Benton, chairman of Encyclopaedia Britannica after he co-founded the New York advertising agency Benton and Bowles, and later U.S. senator from Connecticut, congratulated Maverick "on one of the best pieces the *Sunday Times* will ever publish." Benton welcomed Maverick "to the fraternity of ex-advertising men, men trained in the use of simple words and direct, forthright expression. Your theme is the top theme of all advertising men in their efforts to train the youngsters who have gone wrong in our schools and colleges."[24]

In London, the article landed on the desk of Maverick's counterpart, Oliver Lyttleton, minister of production under Winston Churchill. Maverick was told that Lyttleton "heartily agrees with all you say. . . . Three years of experience in government departments has not made him any more tolerant of official obscurity, and he would like you to know that you have his sympathy." Maverick also received a copy of Lyttleton's 1941 New Year's message to his staff, which began: "I think it surprising that in this Department, which I regard as one of the last temples of Reason in a distracted world, so much pain should be taken by some writers to conceal, rather than to disclose, their meaning." He went on to list examples of what three years later would be called gobbledygook and suggested some short synonyms: "pay" should be substituted for "remuneration," "yes" for "in the affirmative," "because" for "when due consideration is given to the fact that."[25]

For the non-English-speaking world, *gobbledygook* is ranked among the toughest words to translate. London-based Today Translation and Business Services Ltd. gave 1,000 professional translators the task of listing the ten words most difficult to translate from English. Number one came out as "googly (as in cricket)," followed by "Spam (as in tins)," and, third, "gobbledegook (as in Plain English Campaign press releases)."[26]

As a new word, *gobbledygook* succeeded where *dingle-doo* had failed. At birth it cleared the initial hurdles for becoming a successful word, what linguist Allan Metcalf lists as having diverse users, frequent use, and sounding vaguely familiar, without being unobtrusive, overly clever, or outrageous. *Gobbledygook* leapt the ultimate hurdle by remaining in wide use for at least two generations.[27]

An original copy of Maury Maverick's mimeographed memo went into the National Archives. Maverick's relation to the word was so well known that a year before his death in 1954 of a heart condition at the age of fifty-eight he confided to a friend, "I do hope that when I kick the bucket that they will do something else than say I originated that one word."[28]

Maverick needn't have worried. But even he could not have foreseen the realms to which his word would spread. Fifty years later J. K. Rowling, using the British variant spelling, had Harry Potter hear voices "not speaking English or any human language he had ever heard." It was Gobbledegook, "a rough and unmelodious tongue, a string of rattling, guttural noises," the native language of the goblins.[29]

ELEVEN

James Garner, John McCain, and the Ford Motor Company

In 1957 Sam Maverick's grandson George began having problems with his mailbox. It was a standard affair, of gray, galvanized steel rounded on the top with a drop door on the front and, on one side, a square red metal flag to be raised or lowered depending on whether there was mail for the carrier to pick up. Near the flag was the name of the addressee, Maverick, lettered large enough to be visible from the road. The mailbox stood on a post at the foot of the driveway up to the secluded home of George Maverick outside Charlottesville, where he taught in the graduate business school at the University of Virginia.

The trouble was, he recalled, that a TV western series—*Maverick: Legend of the West*—had begun and was rising fast in the Nielsen ratings. Some Charlottesville fans driving by tried getting into the spirit of the Wild West by using the mailbox named Maverick for quick target practice. Soon it was riddled with bullet holes.[1]

George Maverick had to move his mailbox farther from the road. It passed mostly out of danger five years later, as the meteoric rise of the series ended. But the appearance of *Maverick* star James Garner as Bret Maverick, introduction of the Ford

Maverick a decade later, and, finally, designation of John McCain as a "maverick" presidential candidate in 2008 brought curiosity about the word's meaning to new heights.

The word was already familiar on stage and screen. *Maverick* made its possible Broadway debut in 1943 in the musical *Oklahoma!* Rodgers and Hammerstein's opening number "Oh, What a Beautiful Mornin'" had, in its second stanza, all the cattle "standin' like statues," except "a little brown maverick is winkin' his eye." The movie *Oklahoma!* hit theaters in 1955, three years after Wild Bill Elliott starred in the film *The Maverick* and a year before Barbara Stanwyck and Barry Sullivan appeared in *The Maverick Queen*, based on the novel by Zane Grey, father of the western fiction genre.

Not long after Warner Bros. expanded from movies into television, screenwriter Roy Huggins pitched the company a proposal for a series he titled *Maverick*. A maverick, he noted, was originally "a calf who has lost his mother and whose father has run off with another cow," or "anyone who doesn't run with the herd . . . a kind of good-natured, unaggressive nonconformist." The series would star a character Huggins named Bret Maverick after Samuel A. Maverick—"a Texas cattleman renowned for his independence"—and Huggins's oldest son, Bret. Early TV westerns like *Hopalong Cassidy*, *Roy Rogers*, and the *Lone Ranger* featured good guys versus bad guys and were aimed at young viewers. "Adult Westerns" like *Gunsmoke* and *Cheyenne* were pioneering more sophisticated plots featuring, Huggins said, not "a great hero who pulls his gun and wins, but, rather, a guy who uses his mind and gets out of trouble by being smarter than the other guys."[2]

James Garner, right, star of the TV series Maverick, *stopped in San Antonio in 1959 for a card-playing appearance with Maury Maverick Jr.*

When *Maverick* debuted on ABC in September 1957, television historian Ed Robertson reports that it took TV western conventions "and turned them inside out. Its hero was not an altruistic lawman or a noble vigilante but rather a card-playing grafter," not a hero "dedicated to serving the good of his fellow man" but one "dedicated to serving his *own* good," not a total scoundrel but one who "always intends, in the back of his mind, to make up for it."[3]

Nor, unlike the traditional western hero, did Bret Maverick "always come out on top. By the end of any given show, he may find himself broke, swindled, thrown out of town." Screen-writer Huggins sensed that in the late 1950s Americans found themselves in "a nation of security-seeking, contented conform-ists" and needed a character like Bret Maverick tied with the freedom-loving past to identify with and help them break out.[4]

The show, peppered with a humor then uncommon in west-erns, clicked immediately. It was nominated for two Emmys in its first season and won one the following season, for Best Western Series. It rose to sixth place in Nielsen viewer ratings despite appearing Sunday night against competing networks' entrenched favorites like Ed Sullivan, Jack Benny, and Steve Allen. James Garner, then a relatively unknown actor, was cast as Bret Maverick, later joined by a twin brother, Bart Maverick, played by Jack Kelly.[5]

When Garner went on the road to promote the program, he stopped in San Antonio for a card-playing appearance with Maury Maverick Jr., who said he was happy to have the family name connected to the series—unlike some older relatives, who had suggested "putting a stop to it on the grounds that 'our grandfather was not that kind of man.'"[6]

Given the prominence of his late father and his own non-conformities, Maury Jr. had become the go-to Maverick in San Antonio. He picked up a familiar generational mantle by having to explain to the likes of *Dallas Morning News* columnist Frank X. Tolbert that "my great-grandfather, Samuel A. Maverick, was not a cow thief." Maury Jr. served with the Marines in the Pacific during World War II, co-chaired the National Advisory Council of the American Civil Liberties Union, served six years as a liberal Democrat in the Texas House of Representatives,

Among the Maverick TV programs and movies was the 1994 film starring Mel Gibson, Jodie Foster, and James Garner.

represented draft protesters during the Vietnam War, and once gave legal assistance to atheist Madalyn Murray O'Hair. During World War II his father wrote of Maury Jr. to a friend: "He writes me prolific letters on politics, and either the boy got indoctrinated by me before he left or he is the smartest man in the United States. All of his opinions are somewhat violent—and exactly my own. They are so near my own that I hesitate to listen to such radical stuff."[7]

James Garner left *Maverick* after three seasons. The series lasted two more, ending in mid-1962. Once its original screenwriter produced the TV hit *The Rockford Files* (1974–80), with Jim Rockford as a Bret Maverick clone, independent television stations picked up on the characterization and began showing *Maverick* reruns. All three major networks attempted revivals. ABC produced a Sunday night movie, *The New Maverick*

(1978), as a pilot for a potential series, CBS aired *Young Maverick* (1979–80), and NBC brought back James Garner in *Bret Maverick* (1981–82). Dell Comics came out with the quarterly *Maverick*, featuring James Garner as a cartoon character, and partnered with a Mexican company in a series of Spanish-language *Aventura Maverick* comic books.[8]

The concept of a maverick persona stayed current via the silver screen as the nickname Maverick for daredevil naval aviator Lt. Pete Mitchell, played by Tom Cruise in the 1986 Academy Award–winning *Top Gun*. Eight years later Warner Bros. adapted its original TV series in the feature-length movie *Maverick*, starring Mel Gibson as Bret Maverick, Jodie Foster as Annabelle, and the aging James Garner as U.S. Marshal Zane Cooper. It was the biggest film opening of the year.[9]

Meanwhile, *maverick* had taken to the road. The Maverick Sportster was billed as the "world's largest fiberglass-bodied car" when it was unveiled in 1952 by a retired aeronautical engineer, Sterling "Smoke" Gladwin Jr., who lived in Mountain View, California, and named his company Maverick Motors. "Put your own brand on a Maverick!" his brochure urged potential customers, who could order a completely assembled car or buy components in a kit and build the car at home. Like a maverick calf, it was "a sort of motherless sports car"—there were no dealers, though repairs could be done at any Cadillac agency. Components of the first Sportster included a LaSalle chassis, Cadillac motor, Buick fender guards, Lincoln headlights, Studebaker and Mercury dashboard instruments, and Chevrolet license plate frames. It broke with the traditional definition of mavericks as cattle by having a prancing horse as its hood ornament and a hubcap motif of a cowboy on a bucking bronco.[10]

Maverick Motors completed seven Maverick Sportsters between 1952 and 1968, most of them having survived to occasionally star in car shows. In *Motor Trend*, Ken Gross described a Maverick Sportster's appearance early one August morning in 2013: "Show-goers were startled when an enormous bottle-green two-seater swept out of the fog and rolled majestically onto the lawn. A low rumble from its big V-8 and twin plumes of smoke from the burbling exhausts punctuated its presence. Bystanders turned to one another asking, 'What's that?' Most had never seen anything like it."[11]

Gladwin's vehicle manufacturer's license expired in 1968, just as Lee Iacocca and the Ford Motor Company were hatching their own plans for a different type of car. Gladwin might have sold the Maverick name to Ford for a substantial sum rather than letting his use of the name expire as he went on to fiberglass construction in other fields. He later noted that "Ford has adopted 'my' name and there's not a lot I can do with it." But Gladwin was not bitter, just "sorry it should be on the nose of such a tin can."[12]

"Why do you call it Maverick?" Ford asked itself in a glossy brochure as it debuted the Maverick car in 1969. The answer: "Because it is unlike any car . . . home-grown or imported. A maverick is different. It breaks the rules. And Ford's Maverick breaks the rules in your favor. It gives you small car economy and still keeps American driving needs in mind. Like Mustang and Thunderbird, it's a car you'd expect only from a maverick like Ford."[13]

Image makers tied Ford's new compact Maverick to the open range.

Since the 1950s, American carmakers had been scrambling to compete with small foreign imports, particularly the Volkswagen Beetle. In 1960 Ford came out with the Falcon, joining the Chevrolet Nova and Dodge Dart as competitors with foreign subcompacts. Ford's sporty Mustang joined the mix in 1964. But the Falcon could not meet new vehicle safety standards, and in 1969 Ford replaced it with the Maverick, a small two-door economy, six-cylinder sedan priced at just under $2,000.

The Maverick launched the computer age at Ford. Ford Engineering's new corporate computer center did the design work, featuring a long hood and fastback roof inspired by the Mustang, its logo a wild horse at full gallop. Ford's Maverick took the cattle slot, its logo featuring the abstract head of a longhorn nestled into the V of the word. "The Maverick is sound, reliable, all-weather transportation for four/five persons," wrote the automotive editor of *Popular Science*. "It's by no means a sports coupe but a good little utility car. It may not have the mystique or excitement of a foreign car, but it is quiet, fast and stylish."[14]

As Ford launched the Maverick, the July 1969 *Ford Times* traced its name to Sam Maverick. "Despite his prominence in public affairs, it was his rugged, stubborn independence that gave him fame," an article asserted, adding that his unbranded cattle spread the term *maverick* "to include other cattle and even men who were individualistic and chose to go their own way—apart from the herd." The familiar portrait of a white-bearded Sam Maverick ran with the story, but on promotional posters picturing "The World's Great Mavericks"—Einstein, Bonnie and Clyde, Van Gogh, Lady Godiva, and others—Ford transformed Sam's likeness into a maverick of the 1960s, with bushy shoulder-length hair, a black moustache, and a monocle over his right eye.[15]

The Maverick debuted to the national press in April 1969 in Carefree, Arizona, near Scottsdale, where a soundstage complex had recently opened. There it was announced that the first Maverick would be given to Sam Maverick's surviving grandson in San Antonio, retired dairyman James Slayden Maverick, seventy-eight. Jim Maverick had said he would go to Carefree "if they'll let me make a speech." But there was no speech, and he received the keys to his new car the next week at the Ford dealership in San Antonio.[16]

The Maverick's first-quarter sales of 100,000 exceeded initial sales of the Falcon or Mustang, leading Ford to claim the Maverick as "the most successful new car in history." Ford's overall new car sales rose 6 percent at a time when industry sales growth was flat. A four-door model with more room in the rear came out in 1971 and other changes followed, until the compact Maverick was discontinued in 1977 and replaced by the midsize Ford Fairmont, with better handling and fuel efficiency.[17]

Ubiquitous though the term *maverick* may have become as it flashed onto television sets and sped down highways, uncertainty remained over what, in truth, a maverick was. A national debate on the question erupted during the presidential election campaign of 2008.

Description of some politicians as mavericks, first noted in Colorado in the 1880s, was cemented in political lingo during the very maverick tenure of Texas congressman Maury Maverick in the 1930s, and the use continued. In 1981 the *Wall Street Journal* headlined a front-page story, "Capitol Hill Strays: Spiritual Descendants of Old Sam Maverick Enliven the Congress," as "They Wear No Man's Brand." Reporter Dennis Farney described how, on a dreary congressional afternoon, "the tousle-haired figure of Rep. John Burton materialized to transform boredom into chaos." The San Francisco Democrat had taken an unexpected path to opposing a bill, leading Farney to term him "part of a declining breed in Congress: the maverick.... Even the dullest members of Congress, including the old men who regularly fall asleep at committee meetings, do have themes uniquely their own. Even in this increasingly homogenized Congress, where more and more members look like bank clerks, each member does have his own peculiar obsessions. What sets the mavericks apart is that their themes are more peculiarly peculiar."[18]

How much more peculiar than peculiar was Senator John

McCain is a question that arose two decades later, during the presidential election campaign of 2000. That January, Thomas Mallon wrote in the *New York Times* of "some of the biggest moments in that quadrennial contest: 'Who Wants to Be a Maverick?'" Mallon thought Republican senators John McCain of Arizona and Bill Bradley of New Jersey had "come the farthest in their quests for the label," whether or not they deserved it. He went to his Funk & Wagnalls to look up the word and still had trouble seeing "either Mr. McCain or Mr. Bradley as unorthodox in any fundamental way." He also puzzled over how "for months the press has attached the 'maverick' seal almost automatically to each party's main 'challenger,'" even when there was no incumbent running for reelection and there was no one to challenge.

Indeed, Mallon thought "real" mavericks had no business running for president: "Most Republicans eager to recapture the White House wish their mavericks would exit stage right and let the party get on with winning instead of looking weird." Rarely, he said, do mavericks help their parties. He picked the twentieth century's "most authentic maverick candidacy" as Wendell Willkie's in 1940. Barry Goldwater in 1964 and George McGovern in 1972 may have been "ideological mavericks," but they had strong conventional credentials as well, and, as with other maverick candidates, "sooner, rather than later, the infatuation fades."[19]

However shaky John McCain's hold may have been on the maverick label, he nearly upset George W. Bush for the Republican nomination in 2000 and felt it worked well enough to play that card again. In 2008 he sought to rekindle the re-

Debate over meaning of the word maverick *peaked during the presidential campaign of 2008, when Republicans John McCain and Sarah Palin campaigned as "Original Mavericks."*

formist, insurgent spirit that had marked his candidacy eight years earlier, pointing to his several disputes with President Bush over torture policy and campaign finance, to teaming up with Democratic senator Edward Kennedy on an immigration reform bill, and, when he won his party's nomination, to his daring move of pulling Sarah Palin from Alaska to be his running mate. Yet McCain had also supported the president by backing the unpopular Iraq War and mixed his campaign staff with former Bush aides.[20]

Simply being in the Senate for eight more years also made it harder to defend a position as a Washington outsider. John McCain did make some headway in positioning himself as a candidate of change. But promotions and television ads claiming he and Sarah Palin were "the original mavericks" took McCain through a buzz saw of disbelief. Americans got so confused that in 2008 *maverick* placed fourth in Merriam-Webster's annual listing of its top ten most looked-up words.[21]

"The Original Maverick? Not So Fast, John McCain" headlined *Vanity Fair* in a cautionary article. The writer trusted the misguided lore in William Safire's *New Language of American*

Politics, yielding a triple-fault by reporting that Sam Maverick's nonbranding was so because it was inhumane, that he claimed all unbranded cattle, and that range wars followed. The writer did get the idea that the title of Original Maverick had already been taken by a pioneer in Texas. The designation in truth went to an "unconventional Texan," Sam Maverick, echoed National Public Radio's *Morning Edition*, which found itself having to correct its reference to Sam Maverick as a rancher rather than a lawyer, and as a conservative politician rather than "a progressive Democrat."[22]

Other media were not as respectful. "John McCain: Make-Believe Maverick" headlined a *Rolling Stone* piece charging that "far from the portrayal he presents of himself as an unflinching maverick with a consistent and reliable record, McCain has demonstrated an unwavering commitment of taking whatever position will advance his own career." "What Is a Maverick, Anyway?" asked a blogger for the *Huffington Post*. New York City's *The Villager* pronounced "the demise of the word 'maverick'" and suggested replacing it with an uncomplimentary adverb, "McCained." One of its proposed meanings: "referring to the forced betrayal of principles resulting in dangerous conformity." One opponent posted an online image of John McCain's head pasted on the windshield of a wrecked Maverick car in a junkyard. *Maverick* actor James Garner filed for a restraining order against John McCain and Sarah Palin to make them cease and desist from referring to themselves as either Maverick or Mavericks.[23]

National media went on the hunt for opinions from Sam Maverick's progeny. National Public Radio tracked down, in Los Angeles, great-grandson Andrew Lewis Maverick, a retired computer technology professor, who verified the word's proper use. In Michigan, a Lansing newspaper located Amelia Maverick Epler Musser, a fourth-generation descendant and Barack Obama partisan who, with her husband Dan, a Republican, owned Mackinac Island's fabled Grand Hotel. "They've hijacked the name," she declared in a story that ran under the headline "One Mad Maverick."[24]

Most reporters found pay dirt in San Antonio, Sam Maverick's hometown. There the *New York Times* discovered Maury Maverick's daughter, Terrellita. In a Sunday "Week in Review" section the *Times* story—picked up by the British news service Reuters—ran a picture of Sam Maverick and gave the family history back to Puritan Boston. It quoted Terrellita Maverick as insisting that John McCain "is in no way a maverick, in upper case or lower case. It's just incredible—the nerve!—to suggest he's not part of that Republican herd."[25]

The ABC News program *Nightline* went directly to Terrellita Maverick in her cozy home, a classic maverick itself—a dwelling converted from a streetcar purchased in the 1930s by her father when San Antonio shut down its light rail lines. He moved it to a bluff on three acres of what was then the edge of the family's Sunshine Ranch. A front door was cut in the side overlooking downtown San Antonio, and a rock fireplace was installed on the opposite side for the living area, where passengers once sat. The motorman's nook was converted into a kitchen, and the conductor's compartment at the opposite end to a bathroom. A World War II surplus prefabricated hutment was added as a bedroom at the rear. Near a portrait of Franklin Roosevelt, *Nightline* had Terrellita Maverick taking after "maverick" McCain and adding that she thought Sarah Palin "more of a maverick than McCain is."[26]

The *Washington Post* ran a photo of Terrellita Maverick's late brother, Maury Jr., "a Maverick by birthright and a maverick by inclination." *Post* writer Joe Holley, who had known him in San Antonio, repeated Maverick's dictum that "just as not every cola is a Coke and not every tissue is a Kleenex, not every nonconformist is a maverick." Irascibility and irreverence, Holley explained, were key ingredients for a true maverick.[27]

A few enterprising pre-election reporters turned up Sam Maverick's biographer, Paula Mitchell Marks, in Austin. "One was from *Reader's Digest*," she remembered. "I thought they subsequently still garbled the story."[28]

While the media was generally portraying the San Antonio Mavericks as a politically liberal clan, *Forbes* got hold of a local writer who knew the names of many descendants of Sam Maverick who no longer bore the Maverick surname. Some saw their family a little differently. "Most of us are conservative Republicans," said one, Sara McNeel Noble. "There are Democrats and left-wingers kind of sprinkled around here and there, but most of [us] are not like that." Observed her cousin Tom McGaughy, "The very word 'maverick,' even within the family, denotes that everyone has different ideas."[29]

Once the election was over and Barack Obama had won, a letter writer to the *Austin American-Statesman* thought it "ironic or, more precisely, poetic justice" that Maverick County, Texas, had voted for Obama over McCain, 78 percent to 21 percent. Two years later, in 2010, *Newsweek* quoted McCain as denying that he was ever a maverick. "I never considered myself a maverick. I consider myself a person who serves the people of Arizona to the best of his abilities," he told a reporter, even though in a tough but successful senate reelection campaign he

South Carolina senator Lindsey Graham tried picking up the maverick mantle for a boost in his Republican presidential primary run in 2016.

once stood behind Sarah Palin as she urged Arizonans "four times in fifteen minutes to send McCain the Maverick back to Washington."[30]

Whether or not it had to do with John McCain's denials that he was a maverick, the designation in the Senate seemed to be up for grabs. In 2016 South Carolina senator Lindsey Graham made an early though unsuccessful stab for the Republican presidential nomination as "A Maverick for President." The next year the website *FiveThirtyEight* headlined that "The Real Republican Maverick" was Maine senator Susan Collins, "the Republican senator most likely to cross the aisle."[31]

Soon, in an extraordinary maverick trifecta in mid-2017, Collins was joined by a new Republican aisle jumper, Alaska senator Lisa Murkowski, and by reinvigorated maverick John McCain himself in casting deciding votes that defeated their own party's health care bill.

In resisting enormous pressure from fellow Republicans, reported the *Boston Globe*, "Senator John McCain reclaimed his maverick status."[32]

TWELVE

Maverick Meets Poddy and Scrubber

Unbranded cattle are still *orejanos* on ranches in Argentina, and *biguas* in Brazil. In Australia, what's called a maverick in the United States can be anything from a *cleanskin* to a *scrubber*—when one's hiding in scrub brush—or a *micky* if an unbranded young bull or a *poddy* if an unbranded calf. Rustlers who go after them are scorned as *poddy-dodgers*.

As it spilled from the United States, *maverick* may have found few gaps to fill in other nations' range jargon, but as a sort of linguistic shape-shifter it could easily adapt to other uses around the globe. *Maverick* perked along in the United States as a familiar word, if of puzzling origin, for a century, until the early 1960s. But when television, movies, and the Ford car injected strong doses directly into the popular culture, *maverick* soared in an upward trajectory that in four decades saw its use quadrupled in the United States and sent it ricocheting abroad.[1]

No indication of affection for a word may be greater than seeing it bestowed upon a newborn child. More and more babies are being named Maverick. Records gathered by Johnson & Johnson's *BabyCenter* website trace the pattern since 1957. After the Maverick television show premiered that year, annual ranking of Maverick as a newborn boy's name in the United

States jumped from 1,398 to 791. After the show's popularity declined, the popularity of the name also dropped, and it ranked 5,932 by 1984. But as the spate of new TV shows and movies came out the trend reversed, pushing ranking of the name Maverick past the 1,000 mark ten years later and continuing upward to 106 for newborn boys in 2017.

More newborn girls are being named Maverick as well. When first measured for girls in 2006, Maverick ranked 18,600. At the time of John McCain's presidential candidacy the name's ranking among girls broke 10,000. Then, as with boys, it seemed to hit critical mass and has kept rising steadily in popularity, to 1,652 in 2017.[2]

There's more to such popularity than first meets the eye.

Maverick made a simple enough leap from surname to unbranded cattle and on to denoting independent and unconventional. But its burst into ubiquitous use as a brand name around the globe was aided by a set of circumstances quite apart from escaped cattle. *Maverick*'s rapid growth as a noun/verb/adjective in general and as a brand name in particular is substantially due to the auspicious arrangement of its vowels and consonants.

The letters fell together in the mists of medieval England.

Surnames came to England with the Norman Conquest in 1066. Use spread irregularly, and they were dropped and changed at will. But four centuries later most English families had a surname, though phonetic spellings shifted widely as jumbled pieces created ever-new images in a turning kaleidoscope. For one family in southwestern England, the kaleidoscope stopped at Maverick. John Mavery was recorded among the yeomanry of East Devon in 1411. Later came John Merycke. Also believed related were Radford Mauericke, Nodias Madericke, and Peter Mavericke as well as others with surnames spelled Mathericke and Mavareek. In 1573 another relation, Robert Maierwick, appeared on the burial rolls of the ancient parish church at Awliscombe, near the River Otter in the rolling hills twenty miles east of Exeter. Maierwick's sons standardized spelling of their surname as Maverick.[3]

It was a fortuitous decision for corporate specialists four centuries later who were looking for an effective brand name without having to invent one. *Maverick* as finally arranged happens to start with a smooth sound and ends with a snap, and passes a critical branding name test by having fewer than five syllables. It may not begin with a preferred high-point Scrabble letter, but it ends with one, a *K*, the other highs being *J, Q, X,* and *Z.*

As a "borrowed" word, *maverick* cannot flash the mental image of a carefully crafted single-product name like Kleenex, Q-Tip, or Jell-O. But its links to uniqueness and nonconformity offer a flexibility lacking in other borrowed words like *amazon*, suggestive mainly of overwhelming size and fierceness. Maverick can also be tweaked for distinction from other Maverick brand names by dropping a letter, as do Maverik Convenience Stores—"Adventure's First Stop"—in the Northwest and makers of Maverik lacrosse equipment, or by dropping two letters, as do boat-maker Mavrik Marine near Seattle and producers of Mavrik Insecticides.[4]

Commercial use of the word *maverick* often maintains its early association with cattle and the range, particularly in the American West. In the East there are restaurant outliers

The association of mavericks and beef has inspired food establishments from Costa Rica to Dover, England, where young Sam Maverick descendant Maverick Fisher of San Antonio checked one out in 1986.

like Maverick Steaks and Spirits in Litchfield, Illinois, but in the West there's a bigger concentration: Mavericks Steak & Cocktails in Aberdeen and Deadwood, South Dakota; Maverick's Country Bar and Grill in Bend, Oregon; Maverick Restaurant near Phoenix; Maverick Jack's—"Mostly Burgers"—in Burlingame, California; Maverick's Real Roast Beef and Maverick's Wood Grill, both near Minneapolis; Maverick's in Scottsbluff, Nebraska; and the Maverick Saloon south of Anchorage, Alaska, where, found one *TripAdvisor* reviewer, "bartender and bouncer were friendly enough."[5]

The Maverick Grill in Floresville, Texas, is only fifteen miles from Sam Maverick's old Conquista Ranch. Who knows, its ten-ounce Maverick Strip ($12.99) could give you a taste of a descendant of one of the original mavericks.

Elsewhere, foodies find *maverick* loosening its grip on meat alone. Sadly, Maverick Burgers are no longer flipped at the shuttered Mavericks Restaurant at Arenal in the rain forest of Costa Rica or at the vanished Maverick in Dover, England, nor can Indonesians find grilled beef at the onetime Maverick Steak House in Jakarta. Steaks are still featured at the Maverick Cafe in Narrabri in New South Wales, Australia, but it's chicken and thin crust pizza that draw diners to The Maverick in Chandigarh, India. And it's pizza and cocktails in London, where *TripAdvisor* places The Maverick, on Buckingham Palace Road, in the top 20 percent of the city's 18,000 restaurants. In Italy you can enjoy fresh pastries and coffee at the cozy new Maverick Café on a square in Cagliari, capital of Sardinia.

East met West at another Maverick Cafe, this one in San Antonio and now closed, run for many years by Maury

This western long-tail shirt label marks one of Blue Bell's Maverick denim products.

Maverick Huey. In the 1950s former congressman Maury Maverick took on the case of a Chinese immigrant chef, K. A. Huey, who was having trouble getting his son admitted to the United States. When his entry was cleared, the grateful son took the name Maury Maverick Huey and gave his own son the name as well. To bridge San Antonio's Chinese and Mexican cultures the café featured "Chinese and Mexican Food, the Best of Two Worlds," with offerings from Lobster Cantonese to Beef Fajita Taco Delight. As a token of gratitude for Maury Maverick's work, when the café opened in 1991 the entire Maverick family was invited.[6]

Parts of cattle that don't make it onto your plate can end up in the offerings of Oregon's Maverick Leather Company or as the Texas Boot Company's Ariat Maverick Brown Round Toe Cowboy Boots. Maverick also stays linked to the range in California's Peter Grimm's Maverick straw cowboy hats and in a host of western wear outlets around the world, from Santa Fe's Mavericks on the Plaza to Fort Worth's Maverick Fine Western Wear to Australia's Mavericks Western Wear in Brisbane. Ohio's All American Clothing Co. markets AA Maverick Jeans "for those who make their own rules, who know what it takes to forge your own path." Blue Bell's Maverick denims survive as prized vintage clothing. England's Maverick Apparel in Bournemouth, Dorset, goes beyond western wear to outdoor products in general.

Steaks and western gear aside, it's the rapid spread in infinite directions of *maverick* as a common brand name that marks the word as such a phenomenon. Some uses may be partly coincidental, like Madonna's Maverick Records label, created from the names of founders Madonna, Veronica, and Frederick. But more such brand names seek to set enterprises or products apart with a jaunty reference to being unpredictable or out of the ordinary. Notes the website of the Maverick American Eatery & Wine Bar in the heart of San Francisco's Mission District: "Our restaurant celebrates the sprit of Samuel Maverick, a 1800s Texas cattle rancher who refused to brand his herd—forever immortalizing himself as a radical and independent thinker." Says Teresa Salomane, founding manager of Maverick Estate Winery near Osoyoos in British Columbia: "Our name didn't come from a TV show or movie, it's because of its meaning as independent and unconventional."[7]

Many think that *maverick*'s sense of independent behavior can be harnessed to good effect. Organizational psychologists in Britain have developed a "Maverickism Scale" so companies can predict "how maverick personalities can be secret weapons that make businesses successful." In fact, advises the author of *Million Dollar Maverick*, we all possess an inner maverick and can benefit by cutting it loose, as the book's subtitle proclaims: "Forge your own path to think differently, act decisively and succeed quickly."[8]

Maverick telegraphs the sense of unpredictability so sought in sports, where the name has become a favorite for team branding. When Dallas gained a National Basketball Association expansion team in 1980, a radio station's naming contest produced so many votes for Mavericks that the name was chosen. To add to the allure, *Maverick* TV star James Garner was made part of the ownership group. The Dallas Mavericks grew into one of the most valuable basketball franchises, despite grumbling from San Antonians who associated Dallas with corporate conformity more than with being unconventional, and from the nearby University of Texas at Arlington, which had been using Mavericks as its official team name since 1971, though it referred to its players more often as the "Movin' Mavs."[9]

Both Dallas and Arlington went maverick on their team logos by picturing mustangs instead of mavericks. Likewise contradictory are symbols of mustangs used by Kentucky's former Owensboro Mavericks, Buffalo's Medaille College Mavericks, Maryland's Manchester Valley High School Mavericks, the McNeil High School Mavericks of Austin, Texas, and the Madison High School Mavericks in Sam Maverick's hometown, San Antonio.

Getting it right with variations on charging bulls rather than galloping horses are the Minnesota State University–Mankato Mavericks, Colorado Mesa University Mavericks, Kiowa County High School Mavericks in Kansas, and California's High Desert Mavericks in Adelanto, plus, across the border, the Maverick Curling Club in Calgary and, in the Thousand Islands Minor Football League, the Loyalist Mavericks of Kingston, Ontario. The Seacoast Mavericks of Portsmouth,

More than a dozen professional to amateur sports teams use the maverick name, including those at the University of Nebraska Omaha, which sees itself as "willing to go against the grain."

New Hampshire, go with a raging cowboy, while the Maverick Soccer League in Cambridge, England, settles for a soccer ball.

The University of Nebraska Omaha Mavericks drove home their "Maverick Mantra" in a radio commercial: "At UNO we are independent thinkers. Explorers. Risk takers. We are willing to go against the grain, ask the hard questions.... We are agents for change and willing to reinvent the present to achieve the future. We are Mavericks, and we invite you to know the O!"

When you're not playing on a team, you can build self-confidence as well as muscle by heading for Maverick Crossfit in eastern Australia, with its 15,000-square-foot gym in Melbourne and a smaller one in Palm Bay, 1,500 miles north on the Coral Sea. It calls itself "a maverick of the fitness world: unorthodox, independent, and totally unlike anything else on the market." Adventurers can sign up for more than a dozen Maverick Races in the English countryside from Dorset to the North York Moors ("Live like a maverick!"), ski Maverick Mountain at Polaris, Montana, or try the Maverick Roller Coaster in Sandusky, Ohio ("You've heard of the Wild West—now you can ride it!").

Using "maverick technology," designers in England came up with fiberglass Maverick Paddles for whitewater kayaking.

You can aim an arrow with a Maverick Bow, fire a Maverick 88 ("The Working Man's Shotgun"), or shoot on the Hathaway Maverick Pool Table, available at Walmart.

If you've seen the TV shows and movies (don't miss *Maverick*, the Taiwanese entry at New York's Asian Film Festival in 2015), read South Africa's online newspaper the *Daily Maverick* and the many novels and potboilers titled *Maverick*, shuffled Maverick Playing Cards, smoked Maverick Cigarettes, enjoyed Glenfiddich Single-Malt Scotch Whisky distilled by Scotland's "maverick whisky makers of Dufftown," been to the Maverick Music Festival on Maverick Plaza in San Antonio, heard British-born singer/rapper Michael Stafford—better known as Maverick Saber—or listened to the likes of the Miami-based country/rockabilly/Latin band named The Mavericks, for further entertainment there's always Sri Lanka. An undated clipping from the Times of India News Service reports that a group of young male strippers in Colombo call themselves The Mavericks, though they haven't told their parents about it. Whether they wear Maverick Jockstraps marketed in Los Angeles or keep manicured with a Maverick Nail Clipper from Illinois (it doubles as a bottle opener) is not revealed.

A naming on the Pacific Coast's Half Moon Bay, twenty minutes south of San Francisco, itself inspired a succession of new mavericks.

Off the coast, a deep sedimentary reef rising upward toward the surface creates waves that can on occasion crest at more than one hundred feet. A trio of surfers walking the beach in the winter of 1961 happened on such a time. They were the first known surfers to spot the huge waves, nearly invisible from shore. With them was Maverick, a German shepherd, his coat bleached white by sun and saltwater. He belonged to Mac McCarthy, who got him as a puppy during the height of the *Maverick* TV series. The dog liked to paddle out with surfers and retrieve their boards, sometimes leaving teeth marks.

But the waves were a quarter-mile out and too risky for Maverick, so he was tied up while the three went to try the surf. They were outmatched by the huge waves and were easily bounced off their seven-foot boards. "Guys were going all over the place," remembered Alex Matienzo, McCarthy's roommate, who brought Maverick along. "You try to turn, and you're moving quick—the board just doesn't want to stay in the wave." When the three returned and untied the waiting Maverick, they named the spot Maverick's Point as his consolation for not going out. Word of the waves' discovery spread and the name of the place was passed along too, and eventually the waves themselves became known as Mavericks.[10]

In 1999 came an invitational surfing contest now named Titans of Mavericks, intended as an annual event sometime between November and March, when conditions are best for the highest Mavericks. Some years the waves do not break above twenty feet and there are no contests. But when a prediction of high waves is made, two dozen chosen competitors have a few days to get to Half Moon Bay from wherever in the world they happen to be. On the big day, as many as 30,000 spectators glue themselves to Jumbotron screens set up on shore to watch surfers pick a wave, choose a starting spot, and maneuver up and down the wave's face, waiting for its force to recede so that, if they're still upright, they can ride their boards over the top of the wave and glide down its back.[11]

California's legendary Mavericks waves are featured on labels of Mavericks Amber Ale, brewed nearby at the Half Moon Bay Brewing Company.

Others were quick to capitalize on the waves' mystique. Designer Kelly Wearstler named her 22K gold-plated bronze extra-wide bracelet the Maverick Cuff, "inspired by a hybrid California surf culture and surfing the web." A Los Angeles design firm used Maverick Cuff to designate its high-rise denim jeans with wide ankle cuffs. When Apple changed its updated computer operating system name in 2012 from "big cat–based nomenclature"—Tiger, Leopard, Mountain Lion—to names in its home state of California, the first new system was OS X Mavericks.

Two hours south of the Mavericks, in Pacific Grove, the Mavericks Civilian Space Foundation supports rocket motor development by students, including a program at Stanford University, where Mavericks Explorers is "the largest student

The 175th Aviation Company's Mavericks platoon went to war in Vietnam wearing patches with the slogan sat cong— *Kill the Viet Cong—below a wild-eyed bull breathing olive branches of peace.*

project activity on campus." One outlet for Silicon Valley–made Mavericks Skin Care products is "the world renowned Ritz-Carlton Half Moon Bay overlooking the infamous Mavericks surf spot."

The Half Moon Bay Brewing Company has brewed, what else, Mavericks Amber Ale. There are more craft beers at Toronto's Northern Maverick Brewing Co. Far to the west, in British Columbia, is the Maverick Estate Winery. In the southern hemisphere there's the Maverick Wine Company at Tanunda, an hour north of Adelaide in South Australia.[12]

The implication of maverick as unpredictable seems to be disregarded as a name for flying objects intended to be dependable. A U.S. Air Force standby since 1972 is the air-to-ground Maverick missile, also known as the AGM-65. The infrared-guided "silver bullet," made by Hughes Aircraft, is now in arsenals of more than thirty nations. Its first use in massive numbers was during the Gulf War in 1991, when more than 8,000 Maverick missiles were fired and credited as a major factor in the allied victory. In the Vietnam War, the

Mavericks platoon of the 175th Aviation Company was armed with eight assault helicopters. Years later, for surveillance the army ordered the Maverick drone, a "swooper-trooper" made in Florida that can fly up to sixty-five miles an hour.

If you can wait until the twenty-fourth century, you can take a voyage on Federation starship USS *Maverick*, as described on the Internet's *Fandom*, "the largest entertainment fan site in the world." Best to be quick about it when the chance finally arrives, for at some point a subspace distortion will disrupt its warp field, the starboard nacelle—seam of the starship—goes, and the *Maverick* spins out of warp, to be ripped apart by a series of explosions. It's hard to figure just when that happens, for the timeline is altered by the Borg.[13]

It would be a lot safer aboard the US *Maverick*, a humble tugboat plying the northwest coast, or the F/V *Maverick*, a crabbing vessel operating in the Bering Sea. An alternative would be to "Plan and Book Your Maverick Moment" with Maverick Helicopters for flights over the Grand Canyon or a landing in the Hana Rainforest on Maui. Or you could join *maverick*'s final continental migration by taking the M/S *Maverick* out of Christchurch, New Zealand, for a cruise to Antarctica.

Travelers seem never far from a maverick shelter. Should you find yourself in Siberia, you can stay warm at the Hostel Maverick on the outskirts of Irkutsk, an hour north of Lake Baikal and a winding drive from the Mongolian border. You're closer to the water at the twenty-four-room Maverick Hotel on the Black Sea in Vlas, Bulgaria. For a more urban setting there's the Maverick City Lodge in the heart of Budapest. For mountains go to the Maverick Lodge in Japan's Fukushima Prefecture, north of Tokyo.

There are lots of choices in or near the United States: the Maverick Motor Inn on the Trans-Canada Highway in Kamloops, British Columbia; the Maverick Motel in Klamath Falls, Oregon; and a handful of independent, naturally, Maverick Inns—in Chickasha, Oklahoma, and in Texas, in Eagle Pass, seat of Maverick County, and in Alpine ("A Roadhouse for Wanderers"). Texas also offers the Maverick Ranch RV Park in Lajitas, twenty miles west of Maverick Mountain at the edge of Big Bend National Park.

Ford keyed off its U.S. success to market a Maverick compact car in Brazil in the 1970s and sold Maverick compact sport utility vehicles in Australia and Europe from 1998 to 2005. The name pops up on Maverick Motorcycles manufactured in Argentina, on lotions and shampoos made at Laboratorios Maverick down the coast from Barcelona in Spain, in marketing reports on the Chinese economy from Maverick China Research in Singapore, and on Maverick and Wolf Eyewear in London. A shop called Maverick and Jane has introduced gourmet popcorn to Johannesburg, South Africa.

The maverick brand is on Maverick Pet Foods made in Florida, Maverick Chocolates handcrafted in Ohio, Maverick Star Geranium seeds marketed from Illinois, Victorinox Swiss Army Maverick Watches sold from Connecticut, Maverick Kitchen Thermometers from New Jersey, Maverick Desks from Maverick Office Solutions in Ohio and California, Maverick Chairs from Cabot Wrenn in North Carolina ($3,030 each if you choose leather upholstery), and, from Oregon, Harry &

An abundance of maverick consumer products includes the Maverick Henrietta Hen Egg Cooker, which can boil seven eggs or poach four.

David's Maverick Royal Riviera Pears, a little too banged up for gold foil wrapping but "just as juicy and sweet as their more photogenic siblings."

If you want hardy mesquite trees without thorns an inch long, there's a maverick for you: *Prosopis glandulosa Maverick*, a grafted thornless variety of Texas honey mesquite. If you're speared by an old-style mesquite and have a medical emergency, Boston Scientific is standing by with three types of Maverick Catheters, one of them, the Maverick XL Monorail Balloon Catheter, "built for big challenges."

Dipping further into the sciences, Dow AgroSciences Canada produces the water-soluble Maverick Herbicide. Geologists ponder the future of iron ore mining at Project Maverick in Western Australia or the Little Maverick Mining Company's prospects for uranium not far from Maverick Canyon in western Colorado. North Carolina–based Maverick Synfuels manufactures Maverick Oasis, "the first small-scale methane-to-methanol production plant that can be co-located at the source of the methane" (some assembly required).

From there things drift into definitions like polymath Gordon Pask's "Mavericks are machines that embody theoretical principles or technical inventions which deviate from the mainstream of computer development, but are nevertheless of value." Mavericks was picked as the name of "a group of atypical mobile elements" discussed in a scientific journal under the headline "*Mavericks*, a novel class of giant transposable elements widespread in eukaryotes and related to DNA viruses."[14]

◆ ◆ ◆

In the blur one could miss the rare instance of a maverick brand tethered to the Maverick family—Vermont's Maverick Sugarbush, maple syrup and sugar produced by a fourth-generation descendant of Sam Maverick whose branch of the family strayed from Texas back to New England. Though several generations removed from the Maverick surname, Arthur Berndt maintained his Maverick identity, as have so many of his incognito far-flung cousins. For as the Maverick family has contributed to the English language, so has the word shaped the Maverick family itself, preserving not only a tribal identity but providing ready-made expectations for family members' thought and behavior.

"It means someone who's independent and defies convention," one Maverick—Merritt Clements, who said he fit the definition—told Jeremy Hobson, cohost for National Public Radio's *Here and Now*. Hobson was in San Antonio preparing an eleven-minute spot, "What Happens When Mavericks Gather for a Family Reunion?" that aired in June 2015. "What

A National Public Radio technician records The Sons of Maverick, led by Doug McNeel, right, for the Here and Now *coverage in 2015 of a Maverick family reunion in San Antonio.*

does it mean to you to be a Maverick?" he asked some of the more than two hundred family members gathered at an appropriately maverick location, a beer garden run by a venerable German singing society on the southern edge of downtown San Antonio. Though some three-year-olds drew blanks on the meaning of being a Maverick, their older siblings and elders came up with imperatives passed down through generations.

"It means being free and unbranded, being wild and free, and not having to answer to anyone," summarized one of the oldest, Maury Maverick's daughter Terrellita Maverick, eighty-nine. "You are your own self."

The stormy afternoon did not dampen the energy of those

who came, from an assistant professor at American University in Beirut—Doyle Avant III—to a featured dancer with the Joffrey Ballet—Graham Maverick—to Fort Worth–based electrical engineer and inventor Maverick Killian. The majority, though, were from San Antonio, most without the Maverick surname, with a heavy lacing of artists, writers, and lawyers. One attorney, Doug McNeel, provided background music as vocalist and lead guitar strummer of a group called The Sons of Maverick, playing "country, folk, gospel and blues spiced with a Texas flavor." A natural for the reunion was the number about Sam Maverick, titled "His Name Was Maverick."

Mixed with the clamor of hundreds of Mavericks trying to organize themselves for a group photo, Hobson blended in for NPR listeners a line of McNeel's lyrics that caught a core meaning of *maverick* not just for Mavericks but also for countless maverick idealists, realists, and branders throughout the world: "True hearts and free spirits with an independent mind."[15]

NOTES

MFP   Maverick Family Papers
MMB   *Maury Maverick: A Political Biography*
MMM   *Memoirs of Mary A. Maverick: A Journal of Early Texas*
TYE   *Turn Your Eyes Toward Texas: Pioneers Sam and Mary Maverick*

CHAPTER ONE

1. Kyle Gann, "American Mavericks," produced in association with the San Francisco Symphony, http://musicmavericks.publicradio.org/features/essay_gann01.html.

2. John Gould, "The Maverick Who Stood up to the Puritans," *Christian Science Monitor*, May 29, 1987, 30. Gould also made the case in his *Maine Lingo: A Wicked-Good Guide to Yankee Vernacular* (Lanham, MD: Down East Books, 1975), 179. Gould avers that in 1630 Boston Sam Maverick was "the free-thinker, or the odd-ball, he was the 'stray,'" unaffiliated with Puritans but allowed to vote with them. Gould then makes the leap that in later times residents of what became Maine, required to swear allegiance to Massachusetts against their will, "recalled the situation of Maverick, which was not unlike their own." Gould cites no evidence for his conclusion or for how or when such a term for unmarked logs in Maine rivers first occurred, other than asserting it "preceded the meaning of an unbranded calf on the western plains by many years." He dismisses authoritative dictionaries as "quite wrong when they ascribe the term to a Texan." Robert Hendrickson's *Facts on File Encyclopedia of Word and Phrase Origins* (p. 545) is one of the few dictionaries to include

Gould's hypothesis and calls it "a good story" but notes the lack of authority. By giving no independent sources to corroborate or endorse his claims, Gould leaves us with little reason to take his creative assumptions seriously.

3. "maverick," www.alphadictionary.com/articles/eponyms/eponym_list_m.html.

4. Watts, *Dictionary of the Old West*, 206; Ken Greenwald, "maverick," www.wordwizard.com.

5. Anna Matteo, "Maverick, a Truly American Word," June 6, 2015, *VOA Learning English*, http://learningenglish.voanews.com/a/maverick-words-and-their-stories/2807850.html.

6. Albert Huffstickler, "Maverick," *Waterways: Poetry in the Mainstream* 14:9 (Oct. 1993), 55–60.

7. "Maverick," www.merriam-webster.com/dictionary/maverick.

CHAPTER TWO

1. Marks, *TYE*, 250. Estimates indicate that a Galveston land agent named Jacob de Cordova, with financial backing from New Orleans, by 1855 controlled more than a million acres of Texas land. Maverick, however, was distinctive for acting alone and accumulating his impressive holdings by purchasing tracts sometimes as small as 160 acres. His wealth, likewise often overestimated, was also, however, considerable. By 1860 he was among 263 Texans with property worth at least $100,000, today's equivalent of $40 million. By the time of his death ten years later, five years after the end of the Civil War, only 11 Texans had managed to hold onto more than $100,000 in real and personal property, in part because Texas land prices plummeted after the war. Maverick was one of the survivors. His property, worth $177,000 in 1870, today would be worth, unadjusted for later surges in value depending on location, at least $51 million (Marks, *TYE*, 218–19, 250).

2. Marks, *TYE*, 152.

3. Marks, *TYE*, xiii, 86, 193. Sam Jr. went overseas to the University of Edinburgh, Lewis to the University of Vermont and then to the University of North Carolina, which William and George

also attended before transferring to the University of Virginia. Lewis was expelled from the University of Vermont for tampering with a bell in a tower but was reinstated, while Albert was expelled from the University of Virginia, according to family tradition, after performing the rare feat of climbing to the top of a column on the university's Rotunda.

4. Marks, *TYE*, xiii, 250. Maverick even initially joined Sam Houston in opposing Texas secession, but, as his wife wrote in her memoirs, "At last he came to believe the quarrel was forced upon us, and that there was before us an 'irres[ist]ible conflict' which we could not escape, no matter where we turned." He was later named one of the three commissioners to accept surrender of U.S. troops in San Antonio in 1861 (Maverick, *MMM*, 96).

5. Marks, *TYE*, 86, 193, 199, 216. Maverick was also a friend of San Antonio Tejano lawyer and statesman José Antonio Navarro.

6. Marks, *TYE*, 202.

7. Ibid., 263.

8. Ibid., 4.

9. The bridge was named in 2013. Charleston named its new Maverick Street in honor of the family in 1895. In San Antonio, the Maverick family is remembered in the naming of a park, plaza, school, library, street, three downtown buildings, and various historical markers and memorials.

10. Judith Schiff, "The Lone Star Yalies," *Yale Alumni Magazine*, Jan./Feb. 2014, retrieved Sept. 22, 2016, at https://yalealumni magazine.com/articles/3806-the-lone-star-yalies.

11. Ibid., 21.

12. Ibid., 30, 33.

13. Ibid., 33–34.

14. Ibid., 36.

15. Ibid., 52, 54.

16. Ibid., 62.

CHAPTER THREE

1. Maverick, *MMM*, 7. The case for Mary Maverick's *Memoirs*

being "the first true autobiography in Texas" is made by Bert Almon in his *This Stubborn Self: Texas Autobiographies* (Fort Worth: Texas Christian University Press, 2002), 20.

2. Ibid., 6, 7.

3. Marks, *TYE*, 73.

4. Maverick, *MMM*, 11–12.

5. Ibid., 23.

6. Ibid., 23–24.

7. Ibid., 28–29

8. Ibid., 25.

9. Marks, *TYE*, 68, 96–97.

10. Ibid., 108–9.

11. S. A. Maverick to Mrs. S. A. Maverick, Jan. 4, 1845, MFP.

12. Maverick, *MMM*, 68.

CHAPTER FOUR

1. Marks, *TYE*, 132.

2. Maverick, "Reminiscences of Sam Maverick [Jr.]," 24.

3. Ibid., 25; Marks, *TYE*, 143. Sam Jr. remembered riding on the steamer, though it is not mentioned with others in Clay Comer's account of Colorado River navigation, "The Colorado River Raft," published in *Southwestern Historical Quarterly* in April 1949.

4. Maverick, *MMM*, 71. By the 1930s silt from the Colorado River had created a land connection from the town of Matagorda out to the peninsula, dividing the bay.

5. Maverick, *MMM*, 74; Kenneth Hafertepe, "The Texas Homes of Sam and Mary Maverick," *Southwestern Historical Quarterly* 109.1 (July 2005).

6. Maverick, *MMM*, 74; Maverick, "Reminiscences of Sam Maverick [Jr.]," 25.

7. Reginald Wilson, "Charles Nathan Tilton, Privateer with Jean Laffite," https://journals.tdl.org/laffitesc/index.php/laffitesc/article/viewFile/67/57; "Agreement between Charles Tilton & S. A. Maverick," Feb. 9, 1847, MFP. The going rate for land in the area at the

time was just under $1 per acre. Maverick was later offered $50 for the houses on the property, which would leave a land cost of $450.

8. "Agreement between Charles Tilton & S. A. Maverick," Feb. 9, 1847, MFP; Maverick, "Reminiscences of Sam Maverick [Jr.]," 23.

9. Maverick, *MMM*, 74; Mag Pearson to Mary A. Maverick, Feb. 16, 1852, MFP.

10. Maverick, *MMM*, 75.

11. Maverick, "Reminiscences of Sam Maverick [Jr.]," 22–23.

12. Maverick, *MMM*, 76–77; Marks, *TYE*, 145.

13. Marks, *TYE*, 145.

CHAPTER FIVE

1. Durham and Jones, *Negro Cowboys*, 15–19. The description "nominally slave but essentially free" first appears in George Maverick's letter to the editor in 1888 ("Ye Maverick," *St. Louis Republic*, Nov. 24, 1888, section 2, p. 11) and is picked up by J. Frank Dobie in *The Longhorns*, 46. Most prewar African American Texas cowboys lived east of the Nueces River. Farther west, cattlemen could find an adequate supply of vaqueros up from Mexico and also feared that slaves would be close enough to the Mexican border to easily escape.

2. Durham and Jones, *Negro Cowboys*, 13. Famous though Jack may have made him, being identified with the word *maverick* also got Sam Maverick tainted, as having been "negligent" and "disinterested." Jack got remembered, whether accurately or not, as "ignorant of cattle and shiftless," "not wishing to be bothered," even "taken to the bottle" (Burt, *Powder River*, 207; Adams, *Western Words*, 97; Adams, *Old-Time Cowhand*, 157).

3. Dobie, *The Longhorns*, 51.

4. Worcester, *Texas Longhorn*, 24, 88, 92–93; Dobie, *The Longhorns*, 34; M. M. McAllen to Lewis F. Fisher, Nov. 16, 2016.

5. Worcester, *Texas Longhorn*, 5–6, 9, 13–14, 23–26.

6. Dary, *Cowboy Culture*, 9, 147.

7. "Matagorda County, Texas, Brands and Marks, vol. 1, 1837–1874," www.rootsweb.ancestry.com/~txmatago/brands.htm;

"Agreement between Charles Tilton & S. A. Maverick, Feb. 9, 1847,"
MFP; Marks, *TYE*, 161. A common assumption that Sam Maverick's
brand combined the letters MK, as in the current Michael Kors
logo, was made even in a chart of brands published in *Southwestern
Historical Quarterly* (7:126, July 1968). The MK brand was in fact
created by Mary Vance (Mrs. George M.) Maverick for another
ranch in the early years of the twentieth century (A. L. Fenstermaker
to Paula Mitchell Marks, Nov. 4, 1987, MFP). Sam Maverick's own
brand was illustrated by his son in "Reminiscences of Sam Maverick
[Jr.]," 40. In his reminiscences, Sam Maverick Jr. conflated Philip
Love with Charles Tilton as seller of the farm and cattle to his father.
There is no evidence that Sam Maverick followed up either of his new
brands by legally registering them in Matagorda County.

8. Haley, *The XIT Ranch of Texas*, 120–21.

9. Anson Mills, *My Story*, 61–62.

10. Worcester, *Texas Longhorn*, 19, 29–30; Olmsted, *Journey
through Texas*, 101.

11. Gard, *Chisholm Trail*, 14.

12. Maverick, *MMM*, 79.

13. Marks, *TYE*, 151–54; Green, *Samuel Maverick, Texan*, 336–38.

14. Marks, *TYP*, 155.

15. John G. Graham to S. Maverick, Nov. 25, 1849, MFP.

16. Mag Pearson to Mary A. Maverick, Feb. 8, 1852, MFP.

17. Mag Pearson to Mary A. Maverick, July 14, 1852, MFP;
Maverick, "Reminiscences of Sam Maverick [Jr.]," 41.

18. James Stanley to Mr. Maverick, July 24, 1850; James T. Lytle to
Sam'l A. Maverick, Sept. 3, 1850; James T. Lytle to Sam'l A. Maverick,
Sept. 21, 1850; Charles Power to S. A. Maverick, Jan. 31, 1851, all in
MFP; Marks, *TYE*, 161.

19. S. G. Cunningham to S. A. Maverick, Sept. 22, 1851, MFP;
Malsch, *Indianola*, 56.

20. "A friend to Justice," May 1853, MFP. Those mentioned as
having written were named Morrison, Gove, and Worcester.

21. Marks, *TYE*, 169–81. A town named Maverick grew up near
some of Sam Maverick's landholdings in Runnels County in central

Texas in the later nineteenth century. It may have gained a population of more than a hundred, though little now remains other than a cemetery, ruins of the school, and a historical marker.

22. Wm. B. Grimes to S. A. Maverick, Feb. 18, 1854, MFP. By this time DeCrow was focusing on the growing sheep business, having expanded his herd of sheep to more than 1,200 (Paul H. Carlson, *Texas Woollybacks: The Range Sheep and Goat Industry* [College Station: Texas A&M University Press, 1982], 28).

CHAPTER SIX

1. Maverick, *MMM*, 92–93; Maverick, original memoirs ms., March 29, 1854, MFP; Maverick, "Reminiscences of Sam Maverick [Jr.]," 41.

2. S. A. Maverick to Mary Maverick, Apr. 25, 1854, MFP; Olmsted, *A Journey through Texas*, 63; Maverick, *MMM*, 93; Maverick, "Reminiscences of Sam Maverick [Jr.]," 41.

3. S. A. Maverick to Mary Maverick, Apr. 25, 1854, MFP; Maverick, *MMM*, 93; David Roth, "Texas Hurricane History," National Weather Service, retrieved Nov. 16, 2016, at www.wpc.ncep.noaa.gov/research/txhur.pdf. After moving the cattle, Maverick retained ownership of Tiltona (Thomas DeCrow to S. Maverick, Feb. 1, 1857, MFP).

4. Dary, *Cowboy Culture*, 106–13, 123, 191. In the early 1850s some drives were also heading to the goldfields of California.

5. S. A. Maverick to Mary Maverick, May 15, 1854, MFP; Olmsted, *A Journey through Texas*, 370.

6. S. A. Maverick to Mary Maverick, May 15, 1854, MFP.

7. S. A. Maverick to Mary Maverick, Apr. 25, 1854, and May 15, 1854, MFP; Olmsted, *A Journey through Texas*, 274, 370.

8. Maverick, *MMM*, 93; Mary Maverick to S. A. Maverick, May 26, 1854, MFP; A. Toutant to S. A. Maverick, July 18, 1856, MFP. The returnees missed the arrival of Sam and Mary Maverick's son Albert, born some two weeks earlier and the ninth of their ten children; three of their four daughters died before reaching the age of eight.

9. Maverick, "Reminiscences of Sam Maverick [Jr.]," 41.

10.   Marks, *TYE*, 136, 209; S. A. Maverick to Mrs. S. A. Maverick, Jan. 4, 1845, MFP. There are indications that slaves at Maverick's childhood home in South Carolina were loosely controlled as well. Mary Maverick agreed with her father that the institution of slavery "was the greatest curse under which men laboured" (Marks, *TYE*, 175–76).

11.   *Gray Jones Houston et al. vs. Samuel A. Maverick et al.*, Karnes County District Court, Spring Term 1856, MFP. Since Maverick's late sister Elizabeth was survived by minor heirs, the county was obliged to file a legal proceeding and appoint a representative on their behalf. The next year, in the spring of 1856, the representative and the court approved Maverick's survey and the proposed division of the property.

12.   George Maverick to *St. Louis Republic*, Nov. 24, 1888; A. Toutant to S. A. Maverick, July 18, 1856, MFP. Of the 400 cattle driven to Conquista Ranch, 250 had been rounded up on Matagorda Peninsula. If only a third of the 400 were branded, that suggests the branded 120 were from Tiltona and represented what remained of the original stock purchased in 1847.

13.   Marks, *TYE*, 200; Maverick, "Reminiscences of Sam Maverick [Jr.]," 42; A. Toutant to S. A. Maverick, July 18, 1856, MFP.

14.   Mary Maverick to Lewis Maverick, Aug. 10, 1856, MFP.

15.   Maverick, "Reminiscences of Sam Maverick [Jr.]," 42; S. A. Maverick to Leo S. Toutant, Aug. 13, 1856, MFP. Leo replied that the breed of horses was unknown, the hogs had not been seen "for a very long time," and the wagon was "all rotten and rusty" (Leo S. Toutant to S. A. Maverick, Aug. 21, 1856, MFP).

16.   S. A. Maverick to Leo S. Toutant, Aug. 13, 1856, MFP; S. A. Maverick to Mary A. Maverick, Aug. 13, 1856, MFP; Leo S. Toutant to S. A. Maverick, Aug. 21, 1856, MFP.

17.   Maverick personally collected the $2,000 at a bank in New Orleans (S. A. Maverick to Mary A. Maverick, Sept. 30, 1856, MFP).

18.   Marks, *TYE*, 240, 301.

19.   Dary, *Cowboy Culture*, 139; Gene Maeckel, "Beauregard Ranch," *Wilson County News*, Dec. 26, 2012, www.wilsoncountynews

.com/article.php?id=48117&n=wilson-county-history-beauregard
-ranch-spawns-maverick-moniker. Both brothers ended up dropping
the hyphen in their last name to simplify it as just Beauregard.

CHAPTER SEVEN

1. Slatta, *The Cowboy Encyclopedia*, 267–68.

2. Watts, *Dictionary of the Old West*. Another western dictionary lists nearly two dozen granular terms for calves, among them *acorn calf* or *deacon*, a runt; *bum calf* or *buttermilk*, an orphan; *dogie* or *sancho*, a motherless, half-starved calf; *full ear*, one not earmarked; *sleeper*, one earmarked by a rustler but not branded; and *slick*, an unbranded calf (Blevins, *Dictionary of the American West*, 85).

3. Worcester, *Texas Longhorn*, 44, 46, 49–50.

4. Ibid., 50–52, 60.

5. Ibid., 46, 52–53; Christopher Long, "Wilson County," *Handbook of Texas Online*, www.tshaonline.org/handbook/online/articles/hcw12.

6. *Chicago Republican*, Sept. 14, 1867, 3, quoted in *San Antonio Daily Express*, Sept. 28, 1867, 2.

7. "A Northern Correspondent on Texas Cattle Raising," *San Antonio Daily Express*, Sept. 28, 1867, 2. Earlier references to branding mavericks were printed in the *San Antonio Herald* on June 20, 1867, and in the *San Antonio Daily Express* on Aug. 9, 1867.

8. Dobie, *The Longhorns*, 49, 51.

9. Haley, *The XIT Ranch of Texas*, 107; Adams, *Western Words*, 192.

10. Haley, *The XIT Ranch of Texas*, 120; Burt, *Powder River*, 207.

11. Dobie, *The Longhorns*, 55–56.

12. Smith, *War on Powder River*, 59; John W. Davis, *The Johnson County War*, www.wyohistory.org/essays/johnson-county-war. The spelling "Mavorick" got past compiler Albert Barrère in *A Dictionary of Slang, Jargon & Cant*, 46.

13. W. D. Hornaday, *San Antonio Express*, Feb. 27, 1910, in Everett, *San Antonio Legacy*, 19–22. The site of the demonstration was long misremembered as having been Military Plaza.

14.   Robert E. Zeigler, "Cowboy Strike of 1883," *Handbook of Texas Online*, www.tshaonline.org/handbook/online/articles/oec02; M. M. McAllen to Lewis F. Fisher, Nov. 16, 2016.

15.   Edward King, "Glimpses of Texas—I: A Visit to San Antonio," *Scribner's Monthly* 7:3 (Jan. 1874), 327–28.

16.   Siringo, *A Texas Cow Boy*, 43. Assessment of the book's significance is in J. Frank Dobie's preface to the reprint of *A Texas Cow Boy*, ix.

17.   McCoy, *Historic Sketches of the Cattle Trade*, 9. This book's significance is likewise assessed by Dobie in Siringo's *A Texas Cow Boy* reprint, ix.

18.   Mills, *My Story*, 58.

CHAPTER EIGHT

1.   Safire, *New Language of American Politics*, 376–77. The definition is perpetuated in the edition now titled *Safire's Political Dictionary*.

2.   Schele de Vere, *Americanisms: The English of the New World*, 4–5, 211.

3.   Cassidy and Hall, eds., *Dictionary of American Regional English*, 537; "maverick," www.wordwizard.com.

4.   Fanny Kemble Wister, ed., *Owen Wister Out West: His Journals and Letters* (Chicago: University of Chicago Press, 1958), 117; Theodore Roosevelt, "Ranch Life in the Far West," *Century Magazine* 35:4 (Feb. 1888), 507; William Mather, "Campaign Buttons Recall Time When Roosevelt Won Hearts of Cowboys," *Chicago Tribune*, June 26, 1904, http://archives.chicagotribune.com/1904/06/26/page/47/article/campaign-buttons-recall-time-when-roosevelt-won-hearts-of-cowboys. Wister made his notation in 1891.

5.   Farmer, *Americanisms Old and New*, 85.

6.   J. H. Morrison, "Development of American Oil Tankers," *International Marine Engineering* 22:3 (March 1917), 106, retrieved Nov. 16, 2016, at https://books.google.com.

7.   Heather Streets-Salter, *World War One in Southeast Asia: Colonialism and Anticolonialism in an Era of Global Conflict* (New

York: Cambridge University Press, 2017), 111–14, 128–31, 141; "Auke Visser's International Esso Tankers Site," www.aukevisser.nl/inter/id613.htm.

8. Kipling, *Life's Handicap*, 267; James, *Cow-Boy Life in Texas*; Nina Flanagan, "Hervey White, Brief Life of a Maverick Impresario, 1866–1944," *Harvard Magazine*, July–Aug. 2006, http://harvardmagazine.com/2006/07/hervey-white.html; Tad Wise, *hv1*, June 18, 2015, https://hudsonvalleyone.com/2015/06/18/maverick-centennial-the-reconciliation-2/2.

9. David F. Thomson, "Brockman's Maverick," *Book News: A Monthly Survey of General Literature* 20 (Sept. 1901–Aug. 1902), 332.

10. "Young Maverick, the Boy from Nowhere," *Brave & Bold: A Different Complete Story Every Week* 203 (Nov. 10, 1906).

11. John A. Lomax, *Cowboy Songs and Other Frontier Ballads* (New York: Macmillan, 1920), 19, 51; John A. Lomax and Alan Lomax, *Cowboy and Other Frontier Ballads* (New York: Macmillan, 1938).

12. [Cox], *Historical and Biographical Record of the Cattle Industry*, 65–66; Freeman, ed., *Prose and Poetry of the Live Stock Industry*, 628–29.

13. "Texas Spoils, a Royal Scramble for the Offices Already Begun," *St. Louis Republic*, Nov. 14, 1888, section 2, p. 7.

14. Ibid.

15. George M. Maverick, "Mr. Edwin H. Terrell of Texas," *St. Louis Republic*, Nov. 15, 1888, section 1, p. 4; Maverick, *Ye Maverick*, 14. Edwin Terrell may have not become a dispenser of political patronage, but he was a recipient. Harrison appointed Terrell as U.S. minister to Belgium, where his wife, Mary Maverick Terrell, died in Brussels during his tenure.

In his 1905 pamphlet that reprints his letter to the editor, George Maverick sets its publication year at 1889 rather than, correctly, at 1888. The pamphlet also reprints a letter published in the *St. Louis Republic* sent four days after Maverick's first letter by Missouri native and early Texas historian John Henry Brown, who asserted that in the Dallas correspondent's writing "a great wrong, doubtless unintentional, is done to the patriarch of the Maverick family in San

Antonio." Brown's letter adds a few more misstatements to the record, notably that by others' branding of Maverick's yearlings, "in this way his herd, in a few years, virtually became extinct."

Another letter appeared from a writer in Hillsboro, Illinois, identified only as "E," who wrote that he knew the Mavericks while in San Antonio and whose historical statements were mostly correct. He colorfully blasted the correspondent's "unmerited slurs on the Maverick family" by stating that "a more complete tissue of false statements could scarcely be put in the same number of lines" (E., "The Mavericks, Some Interesting Facts Concerning the Great Texas Family," *St. Louis Republic*, Nov. 18, 1888, section 3, p. 23).

16.   George M. Maverick, "'Ye Maverick,' a Term Which All Stockmen Use and Understand," *St. Louis Republic*, Nov. 24, 1888, section 2, p. 11. For good measure, and no doubt to improve the impressions of friends and neighbors misinformed by the dispatch from Dallas, George Maverick added a brief biography of his late father.

17.   Maverick, "Ye Maverick," *St. Louis Republic*, Nov. 24, 1888; Maverick, "Reminiscences of Sam Maverick [Jr.]," 23. George Maverick wrote that "a neighbor being indebted to Mr. Maverick in the sum of $1,200 paid the debt in cattle, transferring 400 animals at $3.00 per head." The only number of cattle specified in the original sales agreement with Charles Tilton is 450, but that was the cap on a final total. The price of $3 a head was to be paid for only as many head as were found up to 450; if only 300 were found the total would be $900, and so on. No record survives of the final number of Tilton's cattle rounded up. Also to be factored into the $1,200 is the sum of $500 specified in the original sales agreement for additional property. Further complicating a specific total of $1,200, in her contemporary, unpublished memoir notes, Mary Maverick put the number of cattle purchased at 450. Only many years later when the memoirs were transcribed, revised, and printed did the number become 400 ("Agreement between Charles Tilton & S. A. Maverick, Feb. 9, 1847," MFP; Maverick, memoir notes, MFP; Maverick, *MMM*, 74).

Given awareness of how unusual the cattle business was in Sam Maverick's career profile, and considering the level of other details provided in his wife's *Memoirs*, one would expect some mention in the *Memoirs* had the cattle been taken only for a debt instead of having been purchased, as she states they were. But with the word in wide use by 1888, the Mavericks could naturally want to find a rationale for the patriarch's negligence with the cattle. Also, the debt rationale of 1888 may have been conflated with the perhaps half-forgotten experience of Sam Maverick's father with cattle in South Carolina much earlier, when a herd of about the same size was taken in payment of a debt (Marks, *TYE*, 145).

A half-century later George M. Maverick's son Lewis A. Maverick, who taught economics at the University of California, made a similar defense in an article in the first issue of *California Folklore Quarterly* (Lewis A. Maverick, "The Term 'Maverick,' Applied to Unbranded Cattle," *California Folklore Quarterly* 1.1 [Jan. 1942], 94–96).

18. Dobie, *The Longhorns*, ix, 46–47. Dobie, as noted earlier, picked up George Maverick's comment that the Mavericks' Matagorda slaves were "nominally slave but essentially free."

19. Peyton, *San Antonio: City in the Sun*, 28.

20. Douglas, *Cattle Kings of Texas*, 61–77.

21. "Slayden in Swan Song Reviews Own Career," *San Antonio Evening News*, Feb. 1, 1919, 5; "Slayden Tells House Why Word Is Used," *Boston Daily Globe*, Feb. 16, 1919, 32, at "How the Mavericks Got Their Name," http://samuelamaverick.blogspot.com/2013/01/origin-of-maverick.html; "Maverick," *Oxford Living Dictionaries*, https://en.oxforddictionaries.com/definition/us/maverick.

22. Twelve letters documenting the tiff date from Nov. 19, 1952, to Jan. 19, 1953, and are in the Maury Maverick Sr. Collection at the Briscoe Center for American History, University of Texas at Austin. That Maverick was furious enough to contemplate legal action is suggested by his comment to the printer that "your continuous libels have the appearance of malice" and by a letter to an old army friend, an attorney in Roswell, New Mexico, whom Maverick asked, "Tell me about this firm."

CHAPTER NINE

1.   Rick Casey, "From Sam of Boston to Our Maury," *San Antonio Express-News*, Jan. 29, 2003, 3-A.

2.   Fischer, *Albion's Seed*, 785.

3.   Cresswell, *Mavericks of Devonshire and Massachusetts*, 33.

4.   Ibid., 41.

5.   Sumner, *A History of East Boston*, 72; Hosmer, *Winthrop's Journal*, 115. Hosmer cites as one indication of Puritan bias a manuscript entry in Winthrop's journal that initially recorded Maverick as "worthy of a perpetual remembrance" for being one of the few ministering to Indians dying of smallpox, but that had the word "perpetual" crossed out by an old pen.

6.   Cresswell, *Mavericks of Devonshire and Massachusetts*, 40.

7.   Sumner, *History of East Boston*, 73, 74; Elizabeth French, "Samuel Maverick," *The New England Historical and Genealogical Register* 69 (1915), 157. The traveler, John Josselyn, was so happy that for several days he took a boat across the harbor to Boston but returned to Maverick's hospitality at night, and came back the next year.

8.   Sumner, *History of East Boston*, 90–91; Greene, *The Negro in Colonial New England*, 16.

9.   Sumner, *History of East Boston*, 82–83, 93–96; Cressy, *Coming Over*, 32.

10.   Sumner, *History of East Boston*, 98–114, 178–82.

11.   Ibid., 128–29; Samuel Maverick, "A Briefe Discription of New England and the Severall Townes Therein," *The New-England Historical and Genealogical Register* 39 (1885), 34–48 (reprinted by Kessinger Publishing, 2010). The manuscript turned up in London at a Sotheby's auction in 1875, was purchased by the British Museum, and was discovered there nine years later by "an experienced American antiquary resident in London" who was employed by the New England Historic Genealogical Society's Committee on English Research. A typical description was for the town of Rowley, where "the Inhabitants are most Yorkshiremen very laborious people and drive a pretty trade, making Cloath and Ruggs of Cotton Wool, and also Sheeps wool with which in few years the Country will about

not only to supply themselves but also to send abroad. This Towne aboundeth with Corne, and Cattle, and have a great number of Sheep." Sudbury he found "a very pleasant place . . . in which I have seen excellent fishing both with hooks & Lynnes and Netts."

12. Sumner, *History of East Boston*, 128; Cresswell, *Mavericks of Devonshire and Massachusetts*, 46.

13. Sumner, *History of East Boston*, 162.

14. Zobel, *Boston Massacre*, 198–200, 348; "Samuel Maverick," www.bostonmassacre.net/players/Samuel-Maverick.htm.

15. Zobel, *Boston Massacre*, 215; *Boston Gazette*, March 12, 1770; "Paul Revere's Engraving," www.gilderlehrman.org/history-by-era/ road-revolution/resources/paul-revere's-engraving-boston-massacre -1770.

16. Stephens, *The Mavericks: American Engravers*, 11–12.

17. Francis S. Berry, *The Scandal of Reform: The Grand Failures of New York's Political Crusaders and the Death of Nonpartisanship* (New Brunswick, NJ: Rutgers University Press, 2009), 63–64. The phrase "To hell with reform!" was first shouted at a campaign rally by Tammany's candidate for district attorney and "captured the spirit of the campaign," wrote Francis Berry, who added that Van Wyck treated it "as a campaign promise and ably fulfilled it."

CHAPTER TEN

1. Henderson, *MMB*, 195.

2. Ibid., 65, 75.

3. Ibid., 83, 134, 145, 271, 304.

4. Henderson, *MMB*, 180, 182–83, 193.

5. Ibid., 214–16, 228–30.

6. Ibid., 216.

7. Ellen Maverick Clements Dickson to Lewis F. Fisher, Jan. 5, 2017.

8. Henderson, *MMB*, 216–17.

9. Maury Maverick [Jr.], "Writing about My Father, a Risk I Want to Take," *San Antonio Express-News*, June 8, 1980, 3-H.

10.   Henderson, *MMB*, 58, 143, 194, 236–38; Maverick, *A Maverick American*, 82–85.

11.   Maverick, *A Maverick American*, 85; Henderson, *MMB*, 101. Maury Maverick was the only southern Democrat in Congress to vote in favor of a federal antilynching law as it went down to defeat in 1937 (Henderson, *MMB*, 140–41).

12.   Henderson, *MMB*, 13, 15–16.

13.   Ibid., 16, 32–35, 39, 152–53; Mencken, *The American Language Supplement II*, 53.

14.   Henderson, *MMB*, 152–53; *Battle Creek Enquirer*, Apr. 2, 1937, 19.

15.   Mencken, *The American Language Supplement II*, 53.

16.   Henderson, *MMB*, 239.

17.   Maury Maverick to Reagan Houston, May 12, 1944, Maury Maverick Sr. Collection, MFP.

18.   "Lengthy Memoranda and Gobbledygook Language," National Archives, https://research.archives.gov/id/7788338.

19.   Jerry Klutz, "The Federal Diary," *Washington Post*, March 30, 1944; and "Gobbledygook Talk," *Cleveland Plain Dealer*, March 31, 1944; Jack Stinnett, "Washington in Wartime," *Duluth News Tribune*, Apr. 29, 1944, all in press scrapbooks, Maury Maverick Sr. Collection.

20.   "Gobbledygook," *Oakland Tribune*, Nov. 18, 1944, press scrapbook, Maury Maverick Sr. Collection.

21.   Maury Maverick to Lester Markel, Apr. 29, 1944, Maury Maverick Sr. Collection.

22.   Maverick, "The Case against Gobbledygook," *New York Times Magazine*, May 21, 1944, 11, 35–36.

23.   Ben Yagoda, "The Strange Saga of Gobbledygook," *Chronicle of Higher Education*, May 5, 2016, www.chronicle.com/blogs/lingua franca/2016/05/05/the-strange-saga-of-gobbledygook; Ralph Keyes, "Is There a Word for That?" *The American Scholar*, Autumn 2013, https://theamericanscholar.org/is-there-a-word-for-that; Henderson, *MMB*, 65; Ayto, *Movers and Shakers*, 121. Origin of the term from the slang "gobble-de-goo" is also a whispered tradition in the Maverick family.

24. William Benton to Maury Maverick, May 24, 1944, Maury Maverick Sr. Collection.

25. Dennis Richter to Maury Maverick, June 19, 1944, Maury Maverick Sr. Collection.

26. David Martin, "Most Untranslatable Word," Nov. 27, 2008, www.todaytranslations.com/news/most-untranslatable-word. Voted hardest word to translate into English was from the Bantu language of Tshiluba—*ilunga*, meaning "a person who is ready to forgive any abuse for the first time, to tolerate it a second time, but never a third time."

27. Metcalf, *Predicting New Words*, 157, 167–68.

28. Henderson, *MMB*, 205.

29. J. K. Rowling, *Harry Potter and the Deathly Hallows* (New York: Scholastic, 2007), 294, 296.

CHAPTER ELEVEN

1. George Maverick to Lewis F. Fisher, personal conversation, August 1968. This George Madison Maverick is not to be confused with his uncle, also named George Madison Maverick, who wrote about the origin of the word *maverick*.

2. Robertson, *Maverick: Legend of the West*, 1, 10–11; Tise Vahimagi, "Maverick, U.S. Western," www.museum.tv/eotv/maverick.htm.

3. Robertson, *Maverick: Legend of the West*, xv–xvi, 4.

4. Ibid., 43, 45. Huggins gave an example: In the "original 'Maverick' pilot, he has a love affair with a beautiful girl, but she's an accomplice in a murder and there's a reward for proving that she's guilty. And Maverick proves it. He turns her over to the sheriff—and then quibbles about the size of the reward! The sheriff, who also loves this girl, says, 'I want you out of this town in ten minutes.' And Maverick says, 'Sheriff, I've gotten out of towns this size in *five* minutes'" (11).

5. Ibid., 43; Vahimagi, "Maverick, U.S. Western," www.museum .tv/eotv/maverick.htm.

6. "'Maverick' TV Star in S. A.," *San Antonio News*, Feb. 16, 1959.

7. Frank Tolbert, "Yale Men Don't Steal Cattle," *Dallas Morning News*, Dec. 1, 1979; Kownslar, *Texas Iconoclast*, 1–2, 19; Maury

Maverick to Reagan Houston, May 12, 1944, Maury Maverick Sr. Collection.

8.   Robertson, *Maverick: Legend of the West*, 282–84, 295.

9.   Ibid., 315–16.

10.   Ken Gross, "Land-Bound Pegasus: The Brief, Fascinating Saga of a Fair-Weather Roadster," Jan. 3, 2014, www.motortrend.com /news/honda-debuts-ev-concept-self-balancing-motorcycle-at-ces; Frederick J. Roth, "Maverick Sportster," www.americansportscars .com/maverick.html.

11.   Gross, "Land-Bound Pegasus." In addition to the seven made by Maverick Motors were an unknown number completed with shells and kits.

12.   Ibid.; Roth, "Maverick Sportster."

13.   "Ford Maverick," undated trifold brochure. A hint of the Old West mixed with the brochure's headline "Goodbye, Old Paint" above the listing of the new Maverick colors, which included "anti-establish mint."

14.   Jan P. Norbye, "Maverick: Ford's Big New Small Car," *Popular Science* 194 (April 1969), 85; "Introduction of the Maverick," *Ford Corporate Studies* no. 7, 3, www.themaverickpage.com/Introduction/ IntrotoMav/introtomav.html.

15.   "Ford's New Maverick," *Ford Times* 62 (July 1969), 21. Sam Maverick got an accurate biography, though the article repeated the inexplicable but sometimes-seen claim that during the Civil War he "served as assistant treasurer of the Confederacy."

16.   Frank X. Tolbert, "Uncle Jim Maverick and the Maverick Car," *Dallas Morning News*, March 10, 1969; "Gets First Maverick," *San Antonio Express-News*, Apr. 26, 1969. Maverick later donated the car to San Antonio's Witte Museum, which displayed it in its Transportation Museum until that subsidiary was closed and most of its collection, including the Maverick car, was disposed of.

17.   "Introduction of the Maverick," *Ford Corporate Studies* no. 7, 1, 4, www.themaverickpage.com/Introduction/IntrotoMav/introtomav .html.

18. Dennis Farney, "Capitol Hill Strays," *Wall Street Journal*, Nov. 12, 1981.

19. Thomas Mallon, "Myth of the Maverick," *New York Times*, Jan. 23, 2000.

20. Michael D. Shear, "McCain Fighting to Recapture Maverick Spirit of 2000 Bid," *Washington Post*, March 15, 2007, www.washing tonpost.com/wp-dyn/content/article/2007/03/14/AR2007031402301 .html.

21. "Lists of Merriam-Webster's Words of the Year," https://en .wikipedia.org/wiki/Lists_of_Merriam-Webster's_Words_of_the _Year#2006.

22. Todd Purdum, "The Original Maverick? Not So Fast, John McCain," *Vanity Fair*, Aug. 6, 2008, www.vanityfair.com/news/2008 /08/the-original-maverick-not-so-fast-john-mccain-dyn/content /article/2007/03/14/AR2007031402301.html; "Original 'Maverick' Was Unconventional Texan," NPR, Sept. 5, 2008, at www.npr.org /templates/story/story.php?storyId=94312345.

23. Tim Dickinson, "John McCain: Make-Believe Maverick," *Rolling Stone*, Oct. 16, 2008, www.rollingstone.com/politics/news/ make-believe-maverick-20081016; Bruce Willey, "John McCain and the Demise of the Word 'Maverick,'" *The Villager*, Oct. 22–28, 2008, http://thevillager.com/villager_286/talkingpoint.html; "James Garner Files Suit against John McCain," *Huffington Post*, www.huffingtonpost .com/steve-young/james-garner-files-suit-a_b_124997.html.

24. "Original 'Maverick' Was Unconventional Texan," NPR, Sept. 5, 2008, www.npr.org/templates/story/story.php?storyId= 94312345; Bill Castanier, "One Mad Maverick," *Lansing City Pulse*, Oct. 29, 2008, 8.

25. John Schwartz, "Who You Callin' a Maverick?" *New York Times*, Oct. 5, 2006.

26. Henderson, *MMB*, 305–6; John Donovan, "These Texas Mavericks Are for Obama," ABC News, http://abcnews.go.com/ Politics/5050/story?id=6090830&page=1.

27. Joe Holley, "A Brand of Politician: To a True Maverick, It's an

Earned Label," *Washington Post*, March 1, 2008, www.washingtonpost
.com/wp-dyn/content/article/2008/02/29/AR2008022903461.html.

28.   Paula Mitchell Marks to Lewis F. Fisher, Apr. 20, 2017.

29.   Jonathan Gurwitz, "Maverick McCain, Biased Media," *Forbes*,
Oct. 24, 2008, www.forbes.com/2008/10/24/maverick-media-bias
-oped-cx_jg_1024gurwitz.html.

30.   Bonnie Maxey, "Maverick Vote," *Austin American-Statesman*,
Nov. 14, 2008, A-12; "McCain the Maverick Fights for His Soul,"
Newsweek, Apr. 2, 2010, www.newsweek.com/mccain-maverick-fights
-his-soul-margolick-70651.

31.   Harry Enten, "The Real Republican Maverick," *FiveThirtyEight*,
https://fivethirtyeight.com/features/the-real-republican-maverick
-maine-sen-susan-collins.

32.   "Murkowski and Collins went maverick long before McCain,"
Boston Globe, July 28, 2017.

CHAPTER TWELVE

1.   Google Books Ngram Viewer, https://books.google.com/
ngrams. Google Ngrams measure frequency of use of words in books
published each year. While that does not reflect frequency of use in
the spoken language or how many times those words are actually read
in the books, they do provide a sense of relative use.

2.   "Maverick," www.babycenter.com/baby-names-maverick-464
505.htm.

3.   Cresswell, *Mavericks of Devonshire and Massachusetts*, 5–12,
24. It was Robert Maierwick's grandson and great-grandson, John
and Samuel Maverick, who first immigrated to Massachusetts. Some
sources speculate that the Maverick surname originated as a form
of Maurice, perhaps in Wales, and has heroic connotations, though
Cresswell found that such a connection is not traceable.

4.   Chi Luu, "What's in a Brand Name: The Sounds of
Persuasion," https://daily.jstor.org/whats-brand-name-sounds
-persuasion; Rich Barton, "Syllables, Scrabble Letters and Picking
Brand Names," http://hopperanddropper.com/syllables-scrabble
-letters-and-picking-brand-names.

5. Other saloons and honky-tonks range from the Maverick Saloon in Santa Ynez, California, to the Maverick Live Country Club in Tucson, to Mavericks Dance Hall in Pflugerville, Texas.

6. Henderson, *Maury Maverick*, 283. The Huey family continues to run San Antonio's oldest Chinese restaurant, Hung Fong, opened by K. A. Huey in 1938, and a second, Ding How.

7. Teresa Salomane to Lewis F. Fisher, May 13, 2017.

8. Elliroma Gardiner and Chris J. Jackson, "Workplace Mavericks: How Personality and Risk-taking Propensity Predicts Maverickism," *British Journal of Psychology* 103:4 (November 2012), 497–519; Knowledge@wharton, "Seems Awkward, Ignores the Rules, but Brilliant: Meet the Maverick Job Candidate," http://business.time.com/2012/08/29/seems-awkward-ignores-the-rules-but-brilliant-meet-the-maverick-job-candidate/3; Alan Weiss, *Million Dollar Maverick* (Boston: Bibliomotion, 2016).

9. Danny Woodward, "In Metroplex: A Tale of Two Mavericks," *ESPN*, May 31, 2011, www.espn.com/espn/page2/story?page=woodward/110531_dallas_mavericks_nickname; Joe Holley, "A Brand of Politician: To a True Maverick, It's an Earned Label," *Washington Post*, March 1, 2008, www.washingtonpost.com/wp-dyn/content/article/2008/02/29/AR2008022903461.html. The name was also used in 1967–69 by Houston's onetime American Basketball Association team.

10. Warshaw, *Maverick's*; "The Selling of a Wave," *SF Weekly*, Oct. 14, 1998, www.sfweekly.com/news/the-selling-of-a-wave; Alexander Haro, "A Short History of Maverick's: Myth, Legend and the Truth Behind the Name," *The Inertia*, Apr. 2, 2015, www.theinertia.com/surf/a-short-history-of-mavericks-myth-legend-and-the-truth-behind-the-name.

11. Alice Gregory, "Life and Death Surfing," *n+1 Magazine* 17 (Fall 2013), https://nplusonemag.com/issue-17/essays/mavericks-surf.

12. Forrest Stroud, "Mac OS X Mavericks," www.webopedia.com/term/m/mac_os_x_mavericks.html.

13. The USS *Maverick*'s future adventures are summarized at http://memory-beta.wikia.com/wiki/USS_Maverick.

14. Jon Bird and Ezequiel Di Paolo, "Gordon Pask and His Maverick Machines," in P. Husbands et al., eds., *The Mechanical Mind in History* (Cambridge: MIT Press, 2008), http://users.sussex.ac.uk /~ezequiel/Husbands_08_Ch08_185-212.pdf; E. J. Pritham et al., "Mavericks," *Gene* 390:1–2 (April 2007), www.ncbi.nlm.nih.gov/pub med/17034960.

15. Jeremy Hobson, "What Happens When Mavericks Gather for Family Reunion," *Here and Now*, June 26, 2015, www.wbur.org/here andnow/2015/06/26/maverick-family-reunion.

SELECTED BIBLIOGRAPHY

MANUSCRIPTS AND ARCHIVES

Maverick Family Papers. Briscoe Center for American History, University of Texas at Austin.

Maury Maverick Sr. Collection. Briscoe Center for American History, University of Texas at Austin.

PUBLISHED SOURCES

Adams, Ramon F. *The Old-Time Cowhand*. New York: MacMillan, 1961.

———. *Western Words: A Dictionary of the American West*. Rev. ed. Norman: University of Oklahoma Press, 1968.

Ayto, John. *Movers and Shakers: A Chronology of Words That Shaped Our Age*. Rev. ed. London: Oxford University Press, 2006.

Barrère, Albert. *A Dictionary of Slang, Jargon & Cant Embracing English, American, and Anglo-Indian Slang, Pidgin English, Gypsies' Jargon and Other Irregular Phraseology*. London: George Bell & Sons, 1897.

Blevins, Winfred. *Dictionary of the American West*. College Station: Texas A&M University Press, 1993.

Burt, Nathan. *War Cry of the West: The Story of the Powder River*. New York: Holt, Rinehart and Winston, 1964.

Cassidy, Frederic G., and Joan Houston Hall, eds. *Dictionary of American Regional English*. Cambridge: The Belknap Press of Harvard University Press, 1996.

[Cox, James.] *Historical and Biographical Record of the Cattle Industry and the Cattlemen of Texas and Adjacent Territory*. St. Louis: Woodward & Tiernan, 1895.

Cresswell, Beatrix F. *The Mavericks of Devonshire and Massachusetts*. Exeter, UK: James G. Commin, 1929.

Cressy, David. *Coming Over: Migration and Communication between England and New England in the Seventeenth Century.* Cambridge: Cambridge University Press, 1987.

Dary, David. *Cowboy Culture: A Saga of Five Centuries.* Lawrence: University Press of Kansas, 1981.

Dobie, J. Frank. *The Longhorns.* New York: Bramhall House, 1936.

Douglas, C. L. *Cattle Kings of Texas.* 1939. Reprint, Austin: State House Press, 1989.

Durham, Philip, and Everett L. Jones. *The Negro Cowboys.* Lincoln: University of Nebraska Press, 1966.

Everett, Donald E. *San Antonio Legacy: Folklore and Legends of a Diverse People.* San Antonio: Maverick Publishing, 1999.

Farmer, John S. *Americanisms Old and New: A Dictionary of Words, Phrases and Colloquialisms Peculiar to the United States, British America, the West Indies, &c., &c.* London: Thomas Poulter & Sons, 1889.

Fischer, David Hackett. *Albion's Seed: Four British Folkways in America.* New York: Oxford University Press, 1989.

Fisher, Lewis F. *San Antonio: Outpost of Empires.* San Antonio: Maverick Publishing, 1997.

Frazier, Irvin. *The Family of John Lewis, Pioneer.* San Antonio: Fisher Publications, 1985.

Freeman, James W., ed. *Prose and Poetry of the Live Stock Industry of the United States.* Denver and Kansas City: National Live Stock Historical Association, 1905.

Green, Rena Maverick, ed. *Samuel Maverick, Texan: 1803–1870.* San Antonio: n.p., 1952.

Greene, Lorenzo Johnston. *The Negro in Colonial New England.* New York: Columbia University Press, 1942.

Haley, J. Evetts. *The XIT Ranch of Texas and the Early Days of the Llano Estacado.* Norman: University of Oklahoma Press, 1953.

Henderson, Richard B. *Maury Maverick: A Political Biography.* Austin: University of Texas Press, 1970.

Hosmer, James Kendall, ed. *Winthrop's Journal: History of New England, 1630–1649.* New York: Charles Scribner's Sons, 1908.

James, W. S. *Cow-Boy Life in Texas, or 27 Years a Maverick.* Chicago: Donohue & Henneberry, 1893.

Kipling, Rudyard. *Life's Handicap: Being Stories of Mine Own People.* London and New York: Macmillan, 1891.

Kownslar, Allan O. *Texas Iconoclast: Maury Maverick, Jr.* Fort Worth: Texas Christian University Press, 1997.

Lomax, John A. *Cowboy Songs and Other Frontier Ballads.* New York: Sturgis & Walton, 1910.

Lomax, John A., and Alan Lomax. *Cowboy and Other Frontier Ballads.* New York: MacMillan, 1938.

Malsch, Brownson. *Indianola: The Mother of Western Texas.* Austin: State House Press, 1988.

Marks, Paula Mitchell. *Turn Your Eyes Toward Texas: Pioneers Sam and Mary Maverick.* College Station: Texas A&M University Press, 1989.

Mathews, Mitford M., ed. *A Dictionary of Americanisms on Historical Principles.* Chicago: University of Chicago Press, 1951.

Maverick, George M. *Ye Maverick: Authentic Account of the Term "Maverick" as Applied to Unbranded Cattle.* San Antonio: n.p., 1905; reprinted by Rena Maverick Green (San Antonio: Artes Graficas, 1937) as *Mavericks: Authentic Account of the Term "Maverick" as Applied to Unbranded Cattle.*

Maverick, Mary A., and George Madison Maverick. *Memoirs of Mary A. Maverick.* Ed. Rena Maverick Green. San Antonio: San Antonio Printing, 1921.

———. *Memoirs of Mary A. Maverick: A Journal of Early Texas.* Ed. Rena Maverick Green and Maverick Fairchild Fisher. San Antonio: Maverick Publishing, 2005.

Maverick, Maury. *A Maverick American.* New York: Civic Frieda, 1937.

Maverick, Samuel, Jr. "Reminiscences of Sam Maverick [Jr.]." Dictated to his daughter Emily Maverick Miller, 1923–29, in Maverick Family Papers, Briscoe Center for American History, University of Texas at Austin.

McCoy, Joseph G. *Historic Sketches of the Cattle Trade of the West and Southwest.* Kansas City: Ramsey, Millett & Hudson, 1874; reprint, Washington, DC: The Rare Book Shop, 1932.

Mencken, H. L. *The American Language: An Inquiry into the Development of English in the United States, Supplement II.* New York: Alfred A. Knopf, 1948.

Metcalf, Allan. *Predicting New Words: The Secrets of Their Success*. Boston: Houghton Mifflin Harcourt, 2002.

Mills, Anson. *My Story*. Washington, DC: Bryan & Adams, 1918.

Morris, William, and Mary Morris. *Morris Dictionary of Word and Phrase Origins*. 2nd ed. New York: Harper & Row, 1988.

Olmsted, Frederick Law. *A Journey through Texas, or, A Saddle-Trip on the Southwestern Frontier*. New York: Dix, Edwards, 1857.

Peyton, Green. *San Antonio: City in the Sun*. New York: McGraw-Hill, 1946.

Robertson, Ed. *Maverick: Legend of the West*. 2nd ed. CreateSpace Independent Publishing Platform, 2012.

Safire, William. *The New Language of American Politics*. New York: Random House, 1968.

Schele de Vere, M. *Americanisms: The English of the New World*. New York: Charles Scribner, 1872.

Siringo, Charles A. *A Texas Cow Boy*. Chicago: M. Umbdenstock, 1885; reprint, New York: William Sloane, 1950.

Slatta, Richard W. *The Cowboy Encyclopedia*. New York: W. W. Norton, 1994.

Smith, Helena Huntington. *The War on Powder River*. Lincoln: University of Nebraska Press, 1966.

Stephens, Stephen DeWitt. *The Mavericks: American Engravers*. New Brunswick, NJ: Rutgers University Press, 1950.

Sumner, William H. *A History of East Boston*. Boston: William H. Piper, 1869.

Warshaw, Matt. *Maverick's: The Story of Big-Wave Surfing*. San Francisco: Chronicle Books, 2000.

Watts, Peter. *A Dictionary of the Old West*. New York: Alfred A. Knopf, 1977.

Worcester, Don. *The Texas Longhorn: Relic of the Past, Asset for the Future*. College Station: Texas A&M University Press, 1987.

Zobel, Hiller B. *The Boston Massacre*. New York: W. W. Norton, 1996.

IMAGE NOTES

The images in this book appear courtesy of the following:

Unattributed images are from the collection of Lewis and Mary Fisher.

INDEX

Among **Lewis F. Fisher**'s books are *American Venice: The Epic Story of San Antonio's River*; *Saving San Antonio: The Preservation of a Heritage*; *San Antonio: Outpost of Empires*; *Chili Queens, Haywagons and Fandangos: The Spanish Plazas in Frontier San Antonio*; and *No Cause of Offence: A Virginia Family of Union Loyalists Confronts the Civil War*. He has received numerous local, state, and national writing awards and was named a Texas Preservation Hero by the San Antonio Conservation Society in 2014.